Francis Reynolds Yonge Radcliffe

The new Politicus

A dialogue concerning the necessity of a national religion

Francis Reynolds Yonge Radcliffe

The new Politicus
A dialogue concerning the necessity of a national religion

ISBN/EAN: 9783337134198

Printed in Europe, USA, Canada, Australia, Japan

Cover: Foto ©Lupo / pixelio.de

More available books at **www.hansebooks.com**

THE NEW POLITICUS

A DIALOGUE CONCERNING THE NECESSITY

OF A NATIONAL ARMAMENT

BEING

THE DEVELOPMENT IN A PLATONIC FORM OF A LECTURE

DELIVERED BEFORE THE CONSTITUTIONAL UNION

ON TUESDAY, MARCH 8, 1881

BY

FRANK R. Y. RADCLIFFE

Of the Inner Temple, Barrister-at-Law
Fellow of All Souls College, Oxford

LONDON
C. KEGAN PAUL & CO., 1 PATERNOSTER SQUARE
1881

NEW POLITICUS.

Intellectus humanus luminis sicci non est, sed recipit infusionem a voluntate et affectibus.'—BACON, *Nov. Org.* i. 49.

WE have probably all of us heard or read at different times many defences of an Established Church and of Religious Education. Such defences are common, but they are, for the most part, of one character. They are addressed to a sympathetic audience. They speak to those who believe in the verities of the Christian Religion and in the necessity of the Establishment, and endeavour to strengthen them in their belief by reminding them of the many blessings and benefits which flow to them from these sources.

B

They postulate the truth which they ought to
demonstrate, and argue that, as Christianity
is the one thing needful, neither State nor
Education can be complete without it. Such
arguments no doubt have their advantage in
the confirming of those who believe. But what
of those who disbelieve—who either regard
Christianity generally as the relic of a decay-
ing superstition, or do not believe in the
efficacy of the particular form of it established
in this country? Can such arguments carry
conviction to their minds? May not the un-
believer say: 'All these blessings and advantages that you speak of depend for their
certainty upon promises contained in a book,
of which we disbelieve the authenticity; written
by an author whom we believe to be an impostor. If you are going to argue from statements contained in that book, you must first
establish its authority.' Having thus de-
molished the 'petitio principii' of the faithful,

they then proceed by the usual argument from expediency, toleration, and equality, to demolish their conclusions and the Establishment.

Perhaps we are all of us too timid about the grounds of our political and religious belief. We assume that in such matters 'the children of this world are in their generation wiser than the children of light.' We fancy that those truths which we most reverence and upon which we acknowledge that our everlasting happiness must depend, inhabit the world of thought, and depend for their reality solely upon the authority of Almighty God Himself. Or, again, we are sometimes apt to resent any attempt to support an institution which we believe to have a divine origin, by arguments drawn from expediency or necessity. We think it beneath the dignity of the cause to seek for such allies. But if we really believe that our religion and Church are of divine origin and sanction, how can we doubt that by this time so goodly a tree should be known by its fruits? If we really wish to persuade others of the necessity of that which we believe—to convert the unbelieving—must we not be content to use arguments which may carry with them a conviction of the *expediency* of our faith, even to those who cannot believe in its *reality*?

My endeavour, then, in these pages, will be to suggest a line of argument to be addressed to those who do not believe in the divine origin of Christianity. I believe that it can be demonstrated, so far as anything political is capable of demonstration, from the results of the past political experience of mankind as recorded in history ;—from the present political experience of each one of us, gathered from our observation of what is every day going on around us ;—from the acknowledged psychological influences by which men, and especially masses of men, are excited or controlled ;—that, whether Christianity itself be true or false, an endowed Christian Church, by law established in any country, is based upon an expediency amounting to necessity. That if such an institution did not already exist, it should be created.

I have said that I shall endeavour to *suggest* a line of argument, because to develop fully such a position would be impossible within reasonable limits ; and a few salient examples are sufficient for my purpose ;—to indicate the direction of the attack, leaving the details to be followed out by the individual commanders.

As regards the form of my argument, I have ventured upon a great experiment, by adopting that of a Platonic Dialogue.

I have done so for this reason. Any argument in support of an Established Church must of necessity rest to some extent upon a

review of the effects of religion upon men's
lives and conduct—a subject which is now-a-
days regarded as the peculiar province of the
preacher.   In the time of Plato it was thought
to be within the sphere of the philosopher
and the politician.   I have some hope that
the familiar Platonic form may avoid what is
one of the chief difficulties in the treatment
of this subject—namely, that flavour of the
pulpit which is uncongenial to political discussion.

It was about two hours after sunset, on a
fine summer evening last year, when our friend
the Politician entered our house and sat down
amongst us.   You know, I believe, the man I
mean, though I dare not mention his name,
lest some informer should make mischief.   He
is, as you know, a true Politician.   Not one so
called, holding some office in the State, who
out of a shallow empiricism provides hurried

remedies for temporary grievances. Our
Politician is a philosopher. He is not wholly
absorbed in the petty facts of his everyday
experience, but has ascended the mountain of
knowledge, and seen the whole world spread
out before him in the light of the sun. He
stands and views, as it were, the country from
afar off, and surveys the entire political horizon
both of the past and present. He is not
frightened by old-world tales about religion
and the gods, nor does he believe in any
particular form of religion, for he is a philosopher. He is swayed by no sectarian or
factional bias, but only by an absolute desire to
rule the State for the common weal. Being,
however, experienced in the events of history,
and the causes of the growth and decay of
nations; knowing that the only way to make
citizens happy and prosperous is to attract
them towards that which is good and true, and
to repel them from that which is evil and false ;

he is curiously absorbed sometimes in the study of the baits and impulses by which men may be led or driven, and every condition or circumstance of life which may tend to their general happiness or misery. These he endeavours to group, and arrange, and to reduce to general principles. And thus he acquires a power of political foresight which enables him to suggest laws for the government of the citizens in the way that is best for themselves and the whole State. He is generally merry and talkative; but on this night he was so reserved and silent that we all cried out upon him, and asked him if he had seen a ghost. 'I have,' said he, 'and have been taught many things that I never before realised.' Whereupon we all asked what manner of apparition this might be, thinking at first that he was laughing at us. But when we saw that he was serious, we begged him to tell us all that he had seen and heard. 'Well,' said he, 'I will tell you; for of all things that have ever happened to me this was the most strange. But be sure you do not whisper it in the city, or men will say that I am mad.'

So we all sat still, and promised that, like the Homeric chieftains, we would 'hold great silence.'

I was walking, said he, upon the edge of the cliff which overhangs the city on its southern side, when I was accosted by a stranger, dressed after the fashion of the reign of Elizabeth. He was of noble mien. His lofty brow was furrowed with care and study, and he looked like one who contemplates things present and to come. In his hand he bore some old-fashioned scientific instruments, with which he appeared to have been conducting an experiment. And while I wondered to see such a man walking upon the surface of the earth, he approached me, as though he had expected to see me there, and

he said: 'What is your meditation?' 'I am
a politician,' said I, 'and I am meditating
upon the art of governing men. I have long
been trying to discover what influences can
be brought to bear upon their hearts, to make
them choose the good and refuse the evil—
how you can persuade men to sacrifice their
own wishes and control their passions, in order
to be virtuous themselves, and to help to
make their fellow-citizens virtuous and happy.
Such I see is the great end of life, and yet I
know of no political power which can be
brought to bear upon men's lives, continuously,
day by day, so that they may form such
habits of virtue and self-sacrifice that the
fascinations of the world of sense cannot entice
them to evil. What power can order the un-
ruly wills and affections of sinful men?'

'I, too,' said he, 'have been a politician;
and I guided my country through perilous
times. I have read many laws both good and

bad ; and have heard many precepts of philosophers. I will open you the book and loose the seals thereof.

'Know you, then,' said he, 'O Politician, a great truth, one which was for a long time overlaid by the fantastic arguments of the schoolmen, but which I unearthed after much patient toil. This truth I taught to men while I lived, and though I am no longer upon the earth, the scientific study of nature is still conducted according to my method. And yet, strange to say, although in the investigation of things inanimate men proceed in this manner ; when dealing with the souls of men, a far nobler material, they neglect the true method, and argue either from general principles which they have not established, or from dogmas of their own faction, which they have learned by rote, and have not examined. Nevertheless, this truth is far more important in the science of politics than in any other

field of knowledge, in proportion as man is a
more noble subject than the beasts or the
elements. Learn then this truth, O Politician,
and have it written in every school in letters
of gold, that the youth of your country may
early imbibe the spirit of true philosophy.
First hear this :

' "Man is but the servant and interpreter
of nature. He can do and understand so much
only as he may have discovered by experiment
or observation in the order of nature ; nor can
he know or do anything further." [1]

' And again : '

' " There is no other means of entering the
kingdom of men, which is founded in philosophy, than there is of entering the kingdom
of Heaven, into which, save as a little child,
it is not permitted to enter." [2]

' If you, O Politician, are willing humbly
to enquire of nature, I will be her interpreter.'

---

[1] Bacon, *Nov. Org.* i. 1.   [2] *Ibid.* i. 68.

'Most willingly,' I replied, 'for the true philosopher is ever willing to learn.'

Then he took me up into an exceeding high mountain, from the edge of which we could see across a deep valley to a dark cliff which towered above us upon the farther side. And as I gazed stedfastly across the valley, wondering what might come to pass, a mist hid the face of the cliff, and when it rolled away I saw the forms of men moving on the surface thereof, as it had been colossal pictures upon the living rock. They seemed to be grouped in scenes, which changed continually, like dissolving views upon a canvas screen.

And as I wondered at this strange appearance, and stood like one who dreams waking, the stranger said to me: 'This, O Politician, is the panorama of the history of the world, and I will be the showman of it. It is in this way that Nature records her experiments upon man, just as your printed books and diagrams record the experiments of men upon the physical phenomena of the earth.'

'Truly,' I replied, 'it is a wonderful show, and one that all our citizens should be brought to see when children.'

'We will let the scenes change,' said the stranger, 'until one appears which is of great interest. For I have always taught that the minds of men are more easily convinced by a few conspicuous instances than by many of less moment.'

Then I looked, and lo! the images passed in continual procession before me, and the stranger expounded their meaning in order.

First I saw a small Arab tribe crossing the river Jordan, and penetrating into Palestine. They were beset by dangers on every side; surrounded and attacked by many tribes more numerous and more powerful than themselves. Yet they drove all before them, and established themselves as conquerors where their forefathers had been but sojourners. I saw them through many centuries still maintain their country and independence, though with varying limits of success, until, under the mighty Solomon, they became the most powerful of all Eastern races. I saw them from that time dwindle and decay, until at length they were carried away captive by another people, and were scattered amongst the nations. And again, many, many years afterwards, I saw them reappear in all their pristine vigour and ferocity, to found anew their ancient capital, and to maintain their independence for a time even against the might of Rome. I saw them fall finally only after a struggle which taxed all the energies of their conquerors. This same tribe I further saw, in after years, scattered throughout all nations, and yet united ; persecuted, and yet prosperous ; pervading all countries, and reaping all fruits ;

supplying the world with energy in every department of art and commerce—great painters, great musicians, great merchants. In everything showing a vigour, a self-denial, a patience under adversity, surpassing that of all other nations.

'And yet,' said I to myself in my musing, 'they were few when they began this conflict; they were few when they were scattered abroad again in after years; they have been Ishmaelites throughout their history, hated of all—whence, then, their extraordinary success?'

'Their religion was their strength,' replied the stranger (for he seemed to hear what I said).

'From the early days when Abraham was called of God, and commanded to leave his home and go, he knew not whither, but went nevertheless, *nothing doubting*, to the Exodus from Egypt; throughout their life as a nation in Palestine, from the days of Joshua

the son of Nun to the Maccabees, they were
ever convinced that "the eternal God was
with them, and underneath were the everlasting arms." In the midst of the fray they
ever saw in fancy the pillar of cloud leading
them on to certain victory. They saw His
mighty hand and stretched-out arm in the
van of the battle, and, confident of success,
they conquered. The staying up of the arms of
Moses by Aaron and Hur was typical of their
entire history. So long as they were fired
with the belief that the God of Israel was
with them, they were successful ; but as their
arms grew tired, and their religion faint, the
enemy prevailed against them. And what was
it in modern days that inspired the despised
nation—the dogs of Hebrews—the accursed
inhabitants of the Ghetto—to fight their way
on through life in spite of every form of persecution, but their religion, their belief in
their destiny ; that, although a cloud was

C

now hanging over them, the day would come when the Son of God, the Messiah, should rise upon their darkness, and they should rule the world ; that it had been promised, and would surely come to pass ? '

'A strange infatuation,' said I ; 'but yet it commanded success.'

Then again I looked, and saw a solitary chieftain of another Arab tribe, armed with a new religion, overthrow the prevailing creeds and superstitions of his own nation, and draw after him from the deserts thousands of fierce warriors, bold in the belief of Islam and its promises of Paradise. I saw him spread a religious and dynastic revolution over nearly the whole of the Eastern world.

The scene changed to Europe, and I saw a single monk, with no reward in his hand but the promises of glory after death, summon round the simple standard of the Red Cross the rapacious, selfish, and turbulent knights of the middle ages. As soldiers of that Cross, they ventured over unknown lands and seas, braving countless dangers, to rescue a Holy Land from an infidel invader.

I saw the simple Swiss peasants kneeling in a body to ask help from God before encountering the overwhelming Burgundian array at the battle of Granson.

I saw the scanty band of Dutch republicans, by endurance and courage such as men had never before witnessed, defeat the great Spanish power, and rescue their freedom, their religion, and their country from the waters in which their heroism had drowned them.

I saw the few but faithful Huguenots following the white plume of Henry of Navarre on the field of Ivry.

I saw Cromwell's 'godly men' praying to God, whilst keeping their powder dry, to smite hip and thigh the riotous crew of Cavaliers. I saw the Covenanting preachers leading their congregations to battle against overwhelming odds. I saw the Pilgrim Fathers forsaking all in their native country for their religion, and going forth, confident in their future, to found a mighty nation.

But I need not weary you by telling of all the scenes that the stranger showed me. These are only a few amongst many.

After a time I turned to the stranger, and I said to him : 'O Stranger, I have learned a lesson of enthusiasm. I see its power to stir men's souls to valiant deeds. But whence is it? How can so few brave the appearance of so great odds?'

'It is on account of their belief in God,' said he. 'Their might is inspired by a confidence that a power superior to all earthly strength will give them the victory, and deliver them from the peril of the sword.'

'It is a strange power, this belief in God,' said I ; 'but yet I know not if it be really a

good thing. It seems to lead men to self-
assertion, bloodshed, and slaughter. But my
citizens, O Stranger, must be gentle, obedient,
and self-sacrificing.'

' Wait a little,' said he, ' until you have seen
further. The vision is not ended. There is
yet another lesson. You have learned as yet
only one thing ; that there is no power under
Heaven that can so impel multitudes of men
to brave danger, pain, and death, as this same
religious enthusiasm. Is it so, O Politician, or
do you yet require instruction ? '

' Not so, O Stranger,' said I, ' for I am convinced already of this first lesson.'

'An apt pupil,' said he ; ' you must surely be
a philosopher. Now let us learn our second
lesson ; and before we look any more at my
show, let us sit down awhile, for your eyes
must be weary with watching, and I will discourse to you a preface.'

Then he sat down, and leaned his brow

upon his hand, and looking blankly into the distance, as one that sees a vision afar off, he continued :

'From among the ranks of that same Arab tribe which we saw in our first picture, which fought so good a fight in the might of the Jehovah in whom they trusted, came forth a new religion—a religion which appealed to no selfish wish or passion of man ; to no love of riches, power, or grandeur ; which from its infancy was the butt of persecution ; which had no comeliness that could be desired of men : no learning in which to clothe itself ; a religion of peasants, artisans and slaves ; whose Author had suffered the death of a common felon. And yet the followers of this religion, in the face of bitter persecution, contempt, stripes, imprisonment, and death, achieved a moral and religious victory over the whole world, and revolutionised society. I will show you some scenes from the history of this religion shortly, O Politician, and do you mark them well. You, being a philosopher, I cannot expect to believe the truth of the facts upon which it is said to be founded ; but being a student of the minds of men, it may interest you to observe its effects thereupon, unreasonable and curious as they may appear. The history past and present of the Hebrews, and the rise of this new religion of which I am now speaking, are perhaps the two most remarkable events in the annals of the world, even apart from their religious aspect, and are well worthy of your consideration.

' Have you not observed,' he continued, 'that the great difficulty of the ruler in dealing with men is to try and induce them to give up what their natural impulses prompt them to seize, for the sake of other people ? '

' No doubt,' said I, ' that is the great problem—in cases, that is to say, when you cannot offer any reward in the future, such as riches or honour, in return for the present sacrifice. And it is in the everyday life of the citizen and in small matters that such habits of self-sacrifice are formed ; and these no political reward or punishment can reach.'

'Most true,' said he ; 'you have well observed. Now, here is the extraordinary power of this religion of which I am now speaking. From the first it has inspired men, contrary to all the strongest appetites and passions of their nature, to deny themselves that which the natural man most desires, and to sacrifice their own dearest wishes for the benefit of others ; to dare that at which their nature trembles, for the benefit of others ; to bear cold, hunger, pain, even death, for the benefit of others ; to live upon earth a life which seems to be bereft of all that could make it pleasant—and all for what ? For the sake of something which their religion promises them in what you would call a vague and doubtful existence after death. And this not in solitary instances, but by hundreds at a time.'

'Ah, I have seen something of this self-sacrifice,' said I, 'for I have some friends, old-fashioned folk, who still believe in what is called the Christian religion, one form of which is established in this country; and they have often explained to me the peculiar views of their faith. And now I think of it, that must be the new religion of which you speak, although I could not at first guess your riddle.

'I must confess it,' said he, 'since I see it is no good dissembling with you.'

'Well,' said I, 'I have been shown by these friends of mine curious instances of self-sacrifice, which they constantly affirm were produced by the working of this religion ; only I thought it was their fancy.'

'Well,' said he, 'we will look at some more pictures, and you will see that, whether

a fancy or whether a fact, this religion has
in times past produced, and still does produce,
the strangest effects upon the lives and conduct of men.'

'I am ready to be convinced,' said I.

And hereupon we returned to our study of
the pictures.

And first I saw the great armies of Friars
who went forth in the early middle ages at the
call of their religion, to fight with sin and
death. Their triple vow alone seemed to be a
renunciation for themselves of all that is
generally considered to be pleasant in this
life. I saw them planting their homes amidst
the filthy, fever-stricken quarters of mediæval
towns, clothing the naked, healing the sick,
feeding the hungry, instructing the ignorant ;
refusing for themselves all reward or comfort
in this life. I then saw thousands of their
followers in after years—men and women,
without name or number, with no ostentation

or pomp of charity—some of them professed, some secular, but all animated with a common purpose—quietly and steadfastly to sacrifice their own lives and comfort for the moral and physical improvement of their fellow-creatures. I saw them working in convents, hospitals, lazar-houses, penitentiaries, prisons, universities, churches and chapels. Wherever were the ignorant, wicked, sick, and poor, there I saw the charitable forms of these Christians.

Indeed, the stranger told me that the founder of this sect had often pointed out this very self-sacrifice as the badge of his true disciples. And when I said to him, 'Surely the origin of philanthropy, as we call it now, is earlier than the introduction of this religion.'

'Not so,' said he. 'Doubtless in the history of the Jews and Moslems up to the present day, and even amongst the heathen of old time, there are to be found many isolated instances of self-devotion for the sake of others

of the same family, tribe, or commonwealth.
But Christian philanthropy is not content
with this. In the first place, it has so far enlarged the sphere of human sympathies as to
hold up as objects of the compassion and
help of the faithful all suffering humanity
of whatever nation or creed under heaven.
The good Samaritan knows of no such distinctions. The mere presence of need, whether
bodily or mental, suffices : he will not pass it
by on the other side. And besides this,
Christianity alone can impel to action whole
classes of people without discrimination as to
age, sex, or station. Bearing in mind these
two characteristics of Christian self-sacrifice, it
is true to say, O Politician, that philanthropy
is of purely Christian origin. The self-sacrifice of heathens, Jews, and Moslems does not
amount to philanthropy, as it is limited both
in its area of operations and in its instruments.
Or, again, if we pass from the origin of philan-

thropy to its development, we can doubtless find solitary instances of marvellous self-devotion amongst other non-Christian men of our own day which are apparently the result of purely humanitarian motives. But of these it may be truly said that, in the first place, such a motive can evidently only appeal to a particular class of mind, from the limited number of such instances. It has no effect whatever upon the mass of mankind. And, secondly, the whole of the humanitarian creed is itself in its origin purely Christian.

'If you wish, O Politician, for examples of what I am saying, you have only to look at our modern philanthropical institutions—our hospitals, dispensaries, asylums, almshouses, universities, and schools. All of these owe their origin entirely to Christianity, and are for the most part conducted even to this day by Christians. Shall we not say, then, O Politician, that true philanthropy without limit either as to its objects, or as to the class of persons whom it impels to action, is purely Christian, at all events in its origin?'

'I must confess it,' said I.

After this we looked on at the scenes for a while in silence, and then he said :

'We have seen now many examples of this form of self-sacrifice ; let us turn and see the devotion of those who, being convinced of the necessity and truth of this religion, have devoted their whole energies and even their lives to teach others what they themselves believe, or to stand forth as living witnesses of its truth.'

Then I looked and saw hundreds of men, women, and even children, pass across the scene, who had devoted their whole lives to preaching, teaching, and bearing witness to the Gospel of their Christianity, in their own lands, or in foreign countries. And this in spite of every form of torture and death, foul climates, savage enemies, hunger, thirst, and nakedness. Many of them I had heard of before, but the significance of their lives had escaped my notice: Paul, Peter, Augustine, the nameless monks who converted the heathen in Europe, Savonarola, Wickliffe, Huss, Jerome of Prague, Thomas More, Las Casas, the two St. Francis, Dominic, Ignatius, and their many devoted followers in Europe and among the heathen in the East and West ; and even in quite recent times, Wesley, Whitfield, Gardiner, and Patteson. And many hundreds of men and women I saw engaged in works of love and charity, whose names I could not discover, for the stranger told me that with their vow of self-sacrifice they had put off all connection with the pleasant world of sense, and even their names, and were known only as Brother or Sister.

Here we interrupted the Politician, for up

to this time we had been entranced by his
story, and had sat drinking in his words with
eyes and ears; and one of us said, being urged
on by the others:

'O Politician, we think that there is no need
of further instances, for we all know many of
these Christians, and have seen with our own eyes
many marvellous examples of this self-sacrifice.'

'Very well,' said the Politician, 'I am not
loth to be interrupted, and, like a pedlar, to
be able to pack up my wares, now that you
have taken your samples. But one thing further struck me as most remarkable in these
men when first I observed them; and that
was that the reason for which they underwent
this self-sacrifice seemed to be so inadequate.
For all that they hoped for was that *after
their death* they would be happy. And when
they were asked upon what ground they based
their belief, they smiled, and said that it had
been promised by the founder of their faith,

and that they were convinced of it, though they gave no reason for their conviction.

'And yet another thing I noticed throughout the whole series of scenes that I saw, which was that the citizens of the States where this Christian religion prevailed were also more vigorous and enterprising in every way than other nations ; and that the periods in the world's history which have been most conspicuous for religious enthusiasm ' have also been most remarkable for enterprise and discovery in literature, art, science, and commerce.

'And, moreover, I noticed that those who were most deeply imbued with this faith were also contented and happy, obedient to command, and loving to others, notwithstanding persecution, adversity, and death. And why again ? Why for this same promise. Because they say that in another world, hereafter, the inequalities that exist here, and which are incurable now, will be redressed ; and therefore it matters not what they suffer here, 'for that the sufferings of this present time are not worthy to be compared with the glory that shall be revealed in them.'

After I had seen all these pictures, and had heard the interpretation thereof, a great light appeared to fall upon me from heaven, and I seemed to have found the very political power that I was seeking when the stranger first accosted me.

And I said to him, 'O Stranger, it has happened with me, as it often happens with us in this life, that I have been seeking afar off for a remedy which was lying close under my eyes the whole time. I wanted to discover a power which could either excite men to action or control them ; which could reach their daily lives, and provide a continual motive for virtue and self-sacrifice, without earthly reward or punishment. And here have I found what I wanted. I see that almost all the great

national commotions which have sprung from
small beginnings, and have revolutionised society, have been inspired by this religious
enthusiasm in some form. Men under its influence will triumph over the most alarming
odds, and court the most fearful perils. One
might almost say that the result of our show
has been to prove that a nation which is fired
by this enthusiasm will invariably outstrip one
which is not, in every sphere of life. Is it not
so, O Stranger?'

'Certainly,' said he, 'when the enthusiasm is
disciplined and orderly.'

'And moreover,' I said, 'and this is the
magician's rod that I was seeking, this Christian religion is the only power which has
ever urged men and women, in any considerable number, to sacrifice themselves for the sake
of others in works of love, peace, and goodwill.

'Yes,' said he, 'there will always be
many impostors, who think to get praise for

themselves by pretending to be followers of this sect, when their heart is far from it. But, speaking of the real Christians, I think you may say that we can prove from history that they alone have, in any considerable number, realised this peaceful habit of self-sacrifice.'

'What manner of power is this,' said I, 'that even those passions of man obey it which no earthly reward or punishment can affect?'

When I said this, the Stranger smiled and said, 'O Politician, you have not yet truly analysed the causes which impel men to action or restrain them. Does it even now seem strange to you that men who thoroughly believe that an Omnipotent Being, who holds all the destinies of the world in His hand, vouchsafes them His protection, should be more courageous than those who think that they have no defence but in their own arm? Is it strange that men who prostrate them-

selves before that Being who they believe will
some day judge them for their deeds com-
mitted upon this earth, and mete out fearful
punishments or ineffable rewards, should hesi-
tate before asking His sanction and help for
a cause which they feel to be unjust or
ignoble? Is it strange that men who thus by
prayer are continually referring their actions
and thoughts to the highest of all imaginable
standards, should act more nobly, uprightly,
and kindly than those who apply no test to
them but that of their own wishes? Or, when
men believe that they and the whole world
were in danger of everlasting punishment, and
that that same Being, of no necessity, but out
of sheer kindness, gave up the position of
God in Heaven to come down upon earth
and undergo ignominious persecution and
death simply to save them from that fate;
that He has said that the only return which
men can make to Him for all this kindness

is to try and imitate Him—is it strange that,
penetrated with a belief in this debt, and this
only price that can be offered in repayment,
they should be willing to sacrifice what, to
them, must appear of little worth in comparison? Is it strange that one writhing in
mortal pain should be comforted by the
thought of endless rest and peace after death?
Or can the undoubted ills of this world be
alleviated by any other antidote? Is it
strange that men who read in a book (which
they believe to be immediately dictated by
God Himself) that they must submit themselves to the rulers that be, and love their
neighbours as themselves, should be better
citizens than those who have no guide but
the natural appetite of man? Is it strange
that a religion which promises to those who
obey it everlasting happiness, such as the
imagination of man cannot picture, should
offer to us in this chequered existence a mo-

tive for good stronger than any mundane or utilitarian ideal? Is it not manifest that it must be so from the constitution of the human mind? Is it not manifest that it is so from the facts of experience? And yet would some banish this same religion from the State, O Politician, saying that it is an effete institution, and one which no longer has power over men.'

'And yet I do not understand,' said I, 'the origin or nature of this power, though I cannot fail to appreciate its results. Perhaps it is a mere phantasy, that will wear out as the world rolls on, and as pure reason gains greater sway. Perhaps it has done its work in the world, and it is no longer necessary either to keep it established as a general example to the nation, or to teach it to the young in our schools. It is so unreasonable and seemingly so capricious.'

'Not so, O Politician,' said the stranger.

'As long as the nature of man remains the same as it now is, so long will enthusiasm, and not the logical faculty, be the chief motive to action, and the power by which great bodies of men are swayed. So long will any idea which can engage the enthusiasm of men on its side be triumphant over the cold unsympathetic dictates of pure reason. This, as we have seen, is the lesson of history, but it has been also the conclusion of philosophy.

'Let me repeat to you an old-world story, drawn from some oracle of ancient Greece, I know not whence, but one which is still fresh, though it was long buried beneath the earth.

'It is said that when man was first brought into the world, the Creator was at a loss to know how to compound his soul, and eventually He compounded it of triple materials, in equal proportions.[1] He made it one-third of the soul of God, one-third of the soul of

---

[1] Plato, *Rep.* ix. 588, 589.

a lion, and one-third of the soul of a serpent. Now, it has been said by a great philosopher of old time that all this is an allegory which aptly describes the existing nature of man's soul. That it is made up of three parts: the intelligence, which is the God-like element; the enthusiasm, which is the lion-like element; and the passions, which are the snake-like element. Of these, two, the God-like and the snake-like, are deadly enemies, and are always trying the one to vanquish the other, so as to make the man whose soul they inhabit their servant. But without the assistance of the lion-like element all their efforts are of no avail, because, being equally matched, the one influence exactly counterbalances the other, and consequently produces no action. Hence the constant struggle of each is to enlist the third or lion-like element on its side. This element is originally neutral, but can be persuaded, by much importunity, to ally itself

with one or the other, and the side which
receives its support invariably prevails, and
impels the man whom they inhabit either to
noble and self-sacrificing or to base and selfish
actions accordingly.

'Consequently, that philosopher affirmed
that the one great end of both legislation
and education is to try and work upon the
enthusiastic side of man's nature, so as to enlist it on the side of the good instincts rather
than the bad. That by this means alone
could the generality of men be brought to
seek that which is good, and avoid that which
is evil, even at the expense of their own
pleasure and comfort. Now, O Politician,
though we may laugh nowadays at the idea
of man's soul being tripartite in origin ; though
we may imagine it to be composed originally
of precisely the same material throughout ;
still this ancient fable is no bad description
of the modes under which the minds of men

present themselves for our observation. Whether originally homogeneous or no, it is certain that now (whether from long transmitted habits or not, we know not) the minds of men *do* present for our observation three distinct characters : the intelligence, the enthusiasm, and the passions. Whether these are mere bundles of motives, differing only in order or arrangement, or actual distinctions in kind in man's mind, again it matters not, for the duty of the politician is not to inquire into the origin of his material, but to deal with it as he finds it. Now, the intelligence of man points out to him that such or such an action is for the good of his fellow-creatures, and that their general good is ultimately his good ; but the passions say, "Never mind the ultimate good, never mind the good of others : it is disagreeable ; choose rather present enjoyment, and let the future and the good of others take care of themselves. Let us eat and drink, for to-morrow we die." Now, here is the task of the moralist and politician : to endeavour to find some power which can work upon the enthusiasm of men, so as to enlist it on the side of the intelligence and against the passions. And have we not found, O Politician, that very power, whether we consider it to be merely "a noble lie"[1] or a stupendous truth ? '

'Certainly we have found it,' said I, 'and I agree with you that the Politician must be content to use his material as he finds it. He has to deal with the results, and not with the causes.'

'There is a wonderful agreement between us,' said the stranger, 'in all this inquiry. Now hear this saying of another great philosopher of old time :—" Pure intelligence by itself can move nothing."'[2]

---

[1] Γενναῖον ψεῦδος: Plato, *Rep.* i. 414.

[2] Ar. *Eth. Nic.* vi. 2, 5 : διάνοια αὐτὴ οὐθὲν κινεῖ.

'Certainly,' said I, 'I cannot resist arguments of such authority.'

'No,' said he, 'you cannot; because they are not mere speculations, but results of the observation of men's minds which are borne out both by our own experience, and that of all time.'

'It is most strange,' said I, 'but it is doubtless true.'

'Ah! my friend,' said the stranger, 'have you never been accosted by a beggar in the street, whose wretched appearance and tale of misery have cajoled alms from you, although your reason told you all the time that he was an impostor?'

'I must confess,' said I, 'that some such thing has happened to me ere now.'

'That is only a small instance,' said he, 'of this law, which is the first principle to be learned by one who wishes to govern men— namely, that the emotions of man, his pity,

his love, his admiration, his natural sympathy
with distress, the lust of the eyes, the magnificence of appearances, the pomp of tradi-
tion—these are the things which kindle man's
enthusiasm, not his intelligence or dialectical
faculty, O Politician, and urge him to action
regardless of consequences, and often in the
very teeth of his reason.'

'Certainly,' said I, 'that has been abun-
dantly proved.'

'And we have also seen,' said the stranger,
'that beyond all comparison, the greatest power
that the world has ever seen to excite men
to love and good works is this *Christian
religion.*'

'Yes,' said I.

'Again,' said the stranger, 'are we not
taught by the experience of the world that
all legislation which attempts to interfere
directly with the daily lives and conduct of
citizens, and to regulate their actions in detail,

has failed, because it is impossible to enforce
it ? '

' Certainly,' said I.

' Must we not, then, at once conclude a
truce with this noble ally—this Christianity,'
said he, ' instead of quarrelling with it and
driving it out of our camp ? '

' I am certain of it,' said I ; ' for thus shall
we obtain a friend who can pass unharmed
through the enemy's lines, and persuade his
men voluntarily to come over to our side.
The world will wonder then at the virtue and
sobriety of our citizens, and go into raptures
over the wisdom of our legislators. And all
the time we shall have shown no invention
whatever, but have merely made use of a
famous political engine, which we found ready
forged to our hands.'

' Just so,' said he, ' we shall obtain credit
under false pretences ; for we have seen—have
we not ?—that this Christianity is, above all, an

influence which pervades the whole life of the man who believes in it, and causes him to form habits of virtue and self-sacrifice, which ultimately become secondary instincts, and make him act from the same motives in the small affairs of daily life as on important occasions.'

'Yes,' said I.

'And, as we have seen,' said he, 'this same Christian motive seems to appeal equally to all classes of minds, gentle and simple, ignorant and refined. In all it produces the same results.'

'Undoubtedly,' said I.

'And this is the influence that we most particularly wanted to discover,' said he.

'It was,' said I.

'And further,' said he, 'being enforced by no external earthly sanction, but only by a man's own conscience, it is a political possibility.'

'Most assuredly so,' said I.

'And yet again,' said the stranger, 'even the bitterest enemies of Christianity admit that our citizens need some influence equivalent to a religion. For those very men who would abolish a religion, so called, which depends for its reality upon the existence of a God, when they come themselves to construct a science of morals or legislation, re-introduce into their own system a very similar principle under the name of philanthropy, humanitarianism, love of nature, love of your fellow-men, or such like appellations.'

'I have often noticed that,' said I.

'But in doing so,' said he, 'they are throwing away a weapon of approved temper for an unreal verbal phantom.'

'So we should say,' I replied; 'but that is not at all their opinion. On the contrary, they are very proud of their systems, and say that they are superior to Christianity, in that

E

they provide a motive for good which is un-selfish, while that provided by Christianity is purely selfish. For, say they, the reason why we affirm that men should be moral and righteous is because by so doing they pro-mote the greatest happiness of the greatest number of their fellow-men. You, on the contrary, dangle before the eyes of your fol-lowers a purely selfish prospect of eternal happiness in return for a temporary self-control. And thus, they say, virtue pro-ceeding from humanitarian motives is meri-torious, while Christian virtue is merely mer-cenary.'

'I admit,' said the stranger, 'that their statements appear at first sight to be plaus-ible : but they are in reality fallacious. They proceed from a false analysis of the real nature of the motives which produce human action. I think we might truly assert, in answer to them, that all motives which produce action in

man are, in their ultimate analysis, at least
self-regarding if not selfish ; that no system
of morality can be complete which does not
supply such motives; that they can only be
supplied by the inducement of a pleasure or
the deterrence of a pain, in some form or
another, either here or hereafter ; and that
Christianity, in its highest development, supplies a motive which is not more, but, if anything, less selfish than that supplied by any
mere system of morality.'

'You are prepared to open fire from a
formidable battery,' said I.

'I am,' said he ; 'but yet I think that one
or two broadsides will suffice ; for, after all,
this is but a feint on the part of our adversary.
The real position that we have to hold is one
of fact. Does Christianity, as a matter of
fact, produce certain results ? How they are
produced is another question. It is only
worth our while just to indicate the manner

in which this objection of the humanitarians
is to be combated—for this reason. Some
men might say that the means by which
these results are produced are evil, and that
the harm done to the human race by the
means is greater than the good produced by
the result.'

'That is possible,' I replied.

'Well, then,' said he, 'we will just sketch
in outline the answer to these objections—for,
indeed, to exhaust the discussion of the subject
would be to institute a complete science of
morals.'

'It would,' I said.

'Let us, then, take my four assertions and
develop them briefly,' said the stranger. 'The
first scarcely needs any support in these days,
since it is now a commonplace of psychology.
So long as man is absolutely content, he is
quiescent. In order to impel him to action
he must be uneasy; and this uneasiness is

produced either by the desire of a pleasure which he has not, or the wish to escape from a pain or discomfort which he has.'

'Certainly,' I said ; 'that is as old as Aristotle.'

'And the second is like unto it,' said he. 'As all human action arises from self-regarding or selfish motives—namely, the desire to obtain a pleasure or to avoid a pain—so it is by means only of a judicious application of such motives that a scientific system of morals becomes possible. Just consider for a moment. The science of morals is that which inquires into and establishes a *summum bonum*, or ideal end of human action and standard of human conduct. But it does not rest there. A mere ideal of conduct would be useless, if men could not be induced to pursue it. Consequently it is essential for a system of morality —if it would provide a practical impetus and guide to moral action—that either its ideal

should be in itself one which incites men to
action, or else that some external sanction
should be applied to enforce the rules of conduct which it dictates. This sanction is supplied, so far as the fundamental laws of society
are concerned, by the penal law of the community, the mere existence of which argues
its need. But what of the minor rules which
should govern the everyday life of the citizen?
If he does not outrage the cardinal laws of
the State or society by flagrant sin, how is he
to be persuaded to sacrifice his own natural
inclinations in the small affairs of daily life,
for the benefit of others? For that is the
object of our search, O Politician!'

'It is,' said I; 'but it is also the philosopher's stone for which these very humanitarians are seeking.'

'Shall we, then, ask them how they sur-
mount the difficulty?' said the stranger.

'I know what their answer will be,' I

replied. 'They will say that a man should be virtuous in even the smallest matters, because by so doing he will promote the greatest happiness of the greatest number of mankind.'

'That, I know, is their hackneyed ideal,' said the stranger, 'but how is it to be attained? Is it in itself so attractive as to draw men towards it as a magnet draws iron? And even if it could do so, would it be by means of a wholly unselfish motive? Is our psychological axiom as to the origin of human action at fault?'

'Certainly not,' I replied; 'for even if it is the inherent nobility and beauty of such an ideal that attracts man towards the path of virtue, it is by reason only of the very law which we have seen to underlie all moral action. It may be that, in some few cases, the pleasure to be derived from doing good to others is so keen that it overbalances the lesser pleasure of immediate personal gratification.'

'Then even in such a case the motive to action is a self-regarding motive,' said the stranger; 'although the mere fact that such a motive should have so powerful an effect upon a man's mind argues the nobility of his nature.'

'It does,' said I.

'Even then in the case of virtuous action proceeding from a purely humanitarian motive,' said he. 'We must amend the usual formula and say : "Such or such a course of conduct tends to the greatest happiness of the greatest number of mankind ; and *that is really your own greatest happiness.*"'

'Yes,' I replied, 'we might remind them of the old myth of the choice of Hercules, which is an excellent illustration of this conflict of rival pleasures, the noble and ignoble, which is ever going on in man's mind.'

'We will admit, then,' said the stranger, 'as, indeed, we have admitted before, that in some rare instances virtuous action may pro-

ceed from a purely humanitarian motive, and
that that is as near an approach to an absolutely unselfish motive as is possible to man;
but it is not a wholly unselfish motive.'

'We will make that admission,' I said.

'But,' said the stranger, 'a science of
morals must not content itself with providing
a motive to action which is suitable only to
a few conspicuous men under particular conditions of nature and education. It must, if
it is to be of any real value, provide a motive
for virtuous action which appeals to all men
alike, whether good or bad, gentle or simple,
learned or ignorant.

'And thus we are brought to the very
point at which mere systems of morality fail
and Christianity triumphs. The utilitarian
ideal is too vague and faint to overcome by
its distant aroma of heavenly pleasure the
coarser scent of present personal enjoyment.
And thus, whatever may be its worth as a

test of the value of moral action, it is useless as a practical guide or incentive to human conduct. It really holds out no inducement for its pursuit. It is only attractive in itself to a very limited class of mind; and it can suggest no external sanction whereby to coerce the moral activity of the less refined and sensitive.

'Now Christianity, on the other hand, appeals to all grades of intelligence and refinement, by providing what we might call progressive motives, which in their highest development are at least as unselfish as that supplied by the humanitarian system.

'In the first place, it holds up an ideal, the same ideal as that of the humanitarian; and then it provides inducements for the pursuit of the ideal graduated according to the class of person to be impelled to action. When dealing with the lowest classes of mankind, who are incapable of action, as a rule, from a chivalrous motive, it doubtless applies a bald system of rewards and punishments. It says to them as a parent says to a young child: " If you do such or such an action, you . will be rewarded: if another, you will be punished." Is it not so?'

' It is,' said I, 'and rightly, for such men do not understand the reason of things, and are, morally speaking, children, and can only be impelled to virtue and deterred from vice by some tangible reward and punishment.'

' That is so,' said he; 'but as we mount the moral scale and deal with the higher order of intelligence, Christianity supplies quite a different motive. It impresses its votary with an overwhelming sense of the debt which he owes to God for his redemption, and thus causes him to pour out all the richest treasures of self-sacrifice without counting either the punishment or the reward, simply out of a chivalrous feeling of generosity

and gratitude. Has not a saint of the Church
well expressed this when he says—

> My God, I love Thee—not because
> I hope for Heaven thereby,
> Nor yet because who love Thee not
> Must burn eternally?'

'I have often admired those lines,' said I,
'but their true meaning had escaped my
notice.'

'Well then,' said he, 'not to waste time—
for it is getting late—let us dogmatise the
result of this digression. And let us say
that moral action can only be produced by
self-regarding motives, and consequently that
no system of morals can be of any service to
mankind in general which does not ultimately
rest upon some system of rewards and punishments; that although such rewards and
punishments must be brought prominently
before the notice of the more degraded of
mankind, who cannot be attracted into the

path of virtue by the mere beauty of an ideal, they gradually fade into the background when we come to deal with a higher order of intelligence and a more sensitive and refined nature; that Christianity in its highest development is as unselfish as humanitarianism, while it acts as a practical moral guide and stimulus to multitudes of human beings, upon whom humanitarianism cannot possibly produce the smallest effect.'

'Those may be regarded as axioms,' said I, 'and indeed, if we had only thought of it, we might almost have spared ourselves the trouble of discussing this point. For, if you remember, the very Philosopher whom you are so fond of quoting undertook in his greatest work to establish a system of morals which should be entirely independent of rewards and punishments. And he promised to show that even if the truly good man received nothing but evil and contumely in this

world and in the next, in return for his virtue,
still it would be better for him to be good. But
he failed egregiously to maintain this position,
and was even driven himself, at the end of
this very work to which I refer, to draw
a picture of judgment after death, in which
those who had been virtuous upon earth were
rewarded, and the evil punished.'

' True,' said the stranger, ' I had forgotten
that.'

' And he was dealing with the highest order
of intelligence only,' said I, ' so that we can
well imagine that he would have agreed cor-
dially with us if he had been constructing a
system to be applied to all mankind.'

' So far, then, so good,' said the stranger. ' We
have surmounted the greatest of our difficulties ;
for we have shown that unless a politician
ignores some of the most obvious characteristics of human nature, he cannot afford
not to recognise Christianity as an all-impor-

tant factor in the well-ordering of his citizens. This is really the corner-stone of our building. If this is once established, the minor difficulties connected with the subject are easily disposed of.

'You may have heard many discussions, O Politician, as to the form of Christian religion which is now established in this country.'

'I have,' said I, 'for many men wish to deprive the existing Church of its pre-eminence as the National Church, and to take away its funded endowments. And I must confess to you, O Stranger, that hitherto I have been rather of their opinion. For it seems to me that to give one form of belief a preference over the others may make some of our citizens jealous and mutinous. And we wish them all to have the same likes and dislikes.'

'Come and let us reason with such men,' said he, 'and show them that it is in the in-

terest of the community that the existing
form of Christianity should remain established.
And let us beg of them, for that reason, to
put aside their jealousies as unworthy of so
great a cause.'

'Let us do so,' said I ; 'if reason leads the
way, they will all follow.'

'Then first,' said he, 'let us speak to those
who say that the Church is too rich, and
that her endowments would do more good if
they were otherwise applied. And let us say
to them : My good sirs, is this nation so poor
that it cannot afford such endowments ? For
if it can afford them, is it possible that money
can be better applied than in endowing an
institution the sole object of which is to make
our citizens virtuous and happy ? If you want
to take away her endowments, you must show
that the nation cannot afford them ; that the
ostensible object to which they are applied is
a bad one ; or that the Church fails to attain

to it. Is not this a sufficient answer for these parsimonious gentlemen, O Politician?'

'Certainly,' said I. 'It would be a sufficient answer to them even if the nation were taxed in order to provide these endowments; and it is overwhelming when we reflect that as a matter of fact no one is taxed one farthing in order to provide the Church's revenues, but they are entirely the result of the voluntary offerings of pious men given for the glory of God at various ages from the earliest days of the Church more than a thousand years ago down to the present time.'

'And now let us turn to those others,' said the stranger, 'who think that, although such money is well spent in the interest of the State, it ought to be provided by the voluntary offerings of the congregations for the time being, and not by the accumulation of past endowments. These are generous men. Let us deal gently with them, and only shoot at them two light shafts, and say : " Do not men complain in all other communions that the ministers are not independent of their congregations ? That having to look to them for their very bread, they often speak and teach what they know will please, and secure large audiences, rather than that which they believe to be true ?" '

' Certainly ; I have often heard that complaint,' said I.

' Then cannot we loose another little arrow, and say : " Do not all men, and not only Christians, nowadays complain that all the educated men in the community are attracted by the hope of wealth and advancement into the large towns, so that the country districts have no high-class resident influence ? Do you not often hear it said that this over-centralisation is destroying the old country-gentleman and yeoman class of the country which used to be its backbone ?" '

'Certainly I do,' said I.

'Then let us turn to our friends and say : " Are not the ministers of the State religion the only antidote now to this evil influence by providing a body of well-born, highly-educated men, to disseminate good influences throughout the country ? And, moreover, is it not notorious that the districts where there is no resident minister of this Church are inferior in morality, education, and order, to the others ? " '

'I have often heard this,' said I.

'Then,' added the stranger, 'by taking away the existing endowments of the Church, you would at once put an end to this body of men ; for few of the country districts are rich enough to support a minister of this class by voluntary offerings.'

'Well,' said I, 'I think you may consider that you have disposed of this point, and have shown that it is better that the ministers should not be dependent upon their congregations for their maintenance. But you have yet to show that it is a good thing that a Church should be established as part of the visible constitution of the country, or that it should be in any way under the control of the State. For one party in our country quarrel with the first of these conditions in the existing Church ; and another and opposite party, with the second.'

'I have not forgotten these two sets of quarrelsome people,' said he. 'Let us first deal with those wno object to the State Establishment of Christianity altogether. And let us speak familiarly to them, and recall to their minds some lessons of their schooldays, which they seem to have forgotten, and let us say, "Have you never observed that if you place a shell in a vessel which is used to boil water, all the calcareous and limy particles contained in the water, and which were previously invisible, are precipitated, and settle on the shell, gradually forming a thick coating all over it, for no apparent reason, unless it were from the mere presence of some definite substance in the water to which the sediment could cling?"'

'Certainly,' said I, 'I have observed it.'

'Well,' said he, 'it is the same with the emotional and sentimental side of man's nature. It floats unobserved on the flood of life until it finds some definite nucleus upon which to settle. And this is one reason why it is so often ignored. It is, to use the hard words of our modern philosophers, a power only energised in reference to some concrete object. Man's love and veneration must have some definite object, embodied in some visible form, round which to cling, or they remain mere abstract feelings, colourless and impalpable. This may be unreasonable, but man is not always a truly reasonable creature; and his unreason is very often more impressionable and more powerful than his reason. Nevertheless, the politician (dealing as he must with the average of mankind and not with the few philosophers) cannot refuse to take into account the power of reverence and enthusiasm, even if associated with mere outward appearances or words.'

'That will be a good argument,' said I; 'but I do not yet see whither you are tending.'

'Why,' said the stranger, 'this truth is quite as important in religion as in any other sphere. Let me again explain my meaning by an example. In a celebrated picture-gallery on the Continent are three pictures which all endeavour to represent Almighty God. One is by a German artist, and that portrays Him as an Emperor; one is by a French artist, and that makes Him a King; and the third is by an Italian artist, and there He is represented as a Pope. Each of these

artists, in thus realising in a concrete form his
abstract idea of God, dresses his skeleton
thought in those attributes which to his mind,
limited by personal and national barriers, are
the outward and visible sign of the greatest
magnificence and power. Does not this, O
Politician, well illustrate how the constitution
of the human mind necessitates the casting of
all our abstractions in a concrete mould, the
configuration of which is determined by the
idiosyncrasies of each individual?'

'Certainly,' I said, 'that is a well-known
truth.'

'Well,' said he, 'almost all religious ideas
are abstractions; and as such abstractions
they cannot be realised by a finite human
intelligence. They must have some concrete
embodiment. And this is the first function
of a National Church and creed, that it provides for the nation such a nucleus. It is by
means of such a Church enthroned with some

pomp of outward display, that religion is
represented in a concrete and intelligible form
to the minds of the nation. Just as to the
individual man the idea of Christianity in the
abstract is vague and unimpassioned, whereas
the idea of Protestantism or Roman Catholicism is definite, sensible, and enthusiastic ;
just as the idea of charity is naturally associated in our minds with some object of pity,
of prayer with some place of worship—so,
too, the national Christian thought finds a
definite expression in our National Church.
For the national Christianity is something
different from the mere sum of the thoughts
and opinions of the individuals composing the
nation. It is the residuum of common Christian sentiment existing in men of all denominations, too much diluted to produce by itself
any perceptible action in the individual apart
from sectarian influences ; but when combined
with like fragments of sentiment in many

others it forms in the aggregate a power in
the State, which has its outward expression in
the National Church. For should a Roman
Catholic or a Nonconformist be asked at this
day whether our nation was a Christian nation,
would he not naturally point to the existing National Church as the best answer to the question ?'

'Certainly he would,' said I.

'Our National Church, then, is to all
Christians of whatever denomination a per-
petual emblem of national faith, and is thus
the rallying-point for all the common Christian
sentiment of the nation, and the best evidence
of its reality.'

'It is,' said I.

'And not only of its reality, but also of
its importance,' he continued. 'It is a continual visible example to men, and especially
to the less educated amongst them, who are
most easily affected by appearances, and are
also those who most need the moral influence

of religion, that that religion is a real practical thing which ought to enter into and sanctify every act of life. Cannot you imagine that the average citizen would at once conclude, if the nation, as such, no longer professed any ostensible belief in Christianity, that Christianity was not so valuable a thing as he had imagined? If the dignitaries of the Church no longer had the high civil position that they now occupy; if the legislators, the judges, and the magistrates of the land conducted their deliberations without, ostensibly at all events, asking for strength and guidance from God in their labours; if the Christian religion were no longer put forward as the figure-head, so to speak, of the constitution, guiding and sanctifying our rulers, do you imagine that the average citizen would regard it with so much reverence? And you must always remember,' he said, ' that I am now considering, not its truth or falsehood, but its effect upon men.'

'Certainly,' said I; 'that I perfectly understand.'

'And then, again,' said he, 'it is by means of an Established Church alone that in these days national worship is possible, and such worship is of the utmost importance. It is in times of great national contrition or rejoicing, when the whole people join together in common humiliation before God, or in common adoration and thanksgiving : when thousands unite in uttering the same litany of penitence or hymn of praise, then it is that religion obtains the most general hold upon the minds of the citizens. They are impressed with the grandeur of the ceremonial, with the responses, like the sound of many waters ; with the sympathetic influence of fellow-worship ; and they go home and con over the scene afterwards in their own minds. The catholicity of the service and the universality of the belief in God amongst their fellow-citizens deepens their personal religious con-

victions for all time. Even reading a description of such ceremonies produces a similar effect
upon men who were not themselves present.
Men are much like sheep in these matters.
The mere herding together of thousands for a
common object produces a depth of conviction
unattainable in a solitary chamber. And how
could this result be obtained in these days,
if there were not one Church and one form of
worship singled out by the State as the representative Church and the representative ritual
of the nation? Amongst the many sects of
Christianity, who would all clamour for the
first place, no common national worship would
be possible.'

'But,' said I, 'surely, O Stranger, in the
days before our Church assumed its present
form, under the supremacy of a secular sovereign, such national worship was even more
common than it now is. How do you account
for that?'

'Very simply,' said he. 'In those days there was practically only one form of religious belief or ritual tolerated throughout Europe. Consequently, on any public occasion, there was no possibility of dispute as to the form the proceedings should take. Now that the Christian sects are so many, matters are quite different.'

'I agree,' said I; 'that had escaped my notice.'

'Well, then,' said he, 'are not these very obvious advantages of an Established Church? It is to a nation what the colours are to a regiment. It serves as a rallying-point and centre for the religious enthusiasm of the entire community. It keeps continually before their eyes a standard, as it were, of possible uniformity— a model of public devotion. Believe me, O Politician, the Christianity of individuals is much more fervent from the mere fact of the example produced by occasional national worship. And the ideas which underlie the Christian religion—charity, peace, and self-sacrifice—are far more easily kept in mind by ordinary men, from the fact that there is always a visible embodiment of that religion before their eyes. And then,' continued he, 'all these reasons apply with double force to our own National Church, from the very fact that it has been long established.'

'That I do not quite follow,' said I.

'It is easy of explanation,' said he. 'Let us go back once more to our schoolroom tale. Do you not remember noticing, O Politician, that the deposit upon the shell could not be produced by any artificial means ; but was the result only of long and gradual natural infiltration ?'

'Certainly,' said I.

'Well, then,' said he, 'let us translate this observation into the world of politics, and say to our opponents : " Have you never observed

that it is only by the long lapse of years and by
the natural association of kindred ideas that particular institutions and offices of the State,
particular robes of office, particular melodies,
and even particular words, gather round them
this deposit, as it were, of reverence, love, and
admiration ? So that men will sacrifice their
fortunes, and even their lives, for the sake of
something which, if you resolve it into its
elements, is little more valuable, at first sight,
than an oyster-shell ? Have you never been
surprised to hear of men dying by hundreds in
defence of the ideas represented by the words
' chivalry,' ' loyalty,' ' honour,' ' liberty,' or
' patriotism ; ' and that often in causes which
in their sober moments they would unhesi-
tatingly condemn ? Have you ever considered
whence these phantoms obtained their dignity ?
Have you never tried to analyse the ' divinity
that doth hedge a king ; ' the awe which pro-
tects a judge ; the emotion produced by a

National Anthem ? Have you ever considered how much of all these ideas which have played so great a part in the world's history are like a brilliant scene upon the stage, a glamour cast over very ordinary mortals by the rosy medium of distant ages through which we are compelled to view them ?" '

' They probably have never analysed these ideas,' said I.

' Well,' said he, ' it is the same with all ancient institutions. By dint of long years it is that they have gradually collected a crust of ideas and associations which, like the tabard of a herald, are handed down to each successive representative, giving him a character quite distinct from, and independent of, his own personality. The wisdom or unwisdom of many generations of citizens has slowly woven a garment, without seam from top to bottom ; and in this they clothe the temporary representative of their institutions, and then do him reverence. The objects of human veneration are not like Nebuchadnezzar's golden image, O Politician. No man can suddenly create a political or social idol, of whatever costly substance, and then bid the peoples, nations, and languages fall down and worship it. "No," say they, "it is only an idol, the work of men's hands." But allow the slow current of national feeling to bring down with it gradually, generation after generation, deposits of sentiment and veneration; and, after a while, an island emerges from the flood, and they say it is a sacred land, the gift of God; and whosoever inhabits it, is holy and entitled to our worship. So do we nowadays take a man; he may be a good man or a bad man, or a very ordinary person. By himself he is like an unwedded queen ant. His working ants pay no attention to him. But we clothe him with a royal robe and crown: we put upon him our seamless coat, a coat of many colours;

and instantly, like the ants when their queen
is wedded, the multitude unites to do him reverence, and would even die in his defence. But
let a man seize perforce such a position, and
they say, " Down with him ! He is a usurper ! "
In short, O Politician, we might say that in
all ages and in all countries the people themselves have unwittingly, and perhaps unreason-
ably, created their own most cherished idols.
And it is notorious, O Politician, to anyone
who has studied our show, that these idols
are of natural growth, and of slow growth, and
that it is impossible to create them artificially,
or to recreate them if once entirely destroyed.'

'There,' said I, 'I entirely agree with you.
Indeed, this fact should be a commonplace of
politics, only one is apt in the heat of discussion, and under the influence of party bias,
to overlook elementary principles.'

'Now, then,' said the stranger, 'let us apply the results of our lesson to our National

Church. It is an ancient institution, more than a thousand years old. It has undeniably become encrusted with the sentiment and veneration of many generations, and now, by the association of ideas, commands the entire veneration and devotion of many thousands of our most orderly and well-conducted citizens. It is now the recognised, enthroned embodiment of our national religion; and as such is also the living standard and witness of the religion and morality of each individual who believes in Christianity, and in a degree, though perhaps unconsciously, to those who have discarded that belief.

'Should anyone doubt its living power, let the munificent gifts of recent benefactors bear witness to the contrary.

'Shall we, then, cast down from its niche an object of veneration of multitudes of people, in all probability shattering it into a thousand fragments? Shall we destroy irreparably the living witness of the greatest moral and political influence that exists amongst us, without overwhelming reasons? For remember, O Politician, that when once destroyed it can never be replaced.

And after all, my friend,' he continued, ' what are the reasons which are offered for this act of Vandalism by its promoters?'

'So far as I have heard,' said I, 'their chief arguments are these: that the existing Church cannot properly be called a National Church, because it is not the Church of the entire nation, or even of a substantial majority of the nation; and that it is unfair to the ministers of other denominations that those belonging to the State Church should monopolise all social and political pre-eminence.'

'We can reply to such arguments, or rather assertions,' said the stranger, ' first by an argument, and secondly by a rebuke. And first let us ask such antagonists what proof they offer of their assertions.

'Can there be a surer sign, we may ask, that the Church does represent the nation than the fact that it exists? Could not the nation at any time destroy it if it were so willed? Would it not die of inanition? Surely, it is for our opponents, in the face of the fact of its establishment, to show that nevertheless it is not national and representative.'

'Certainly,' said I.

'But yet we need not insist upon our strict rights in such a cause,' said he, 'and we will undertake, if they will explain what they mean by representative or national, to show that our existing Church is both.'

'It is best to be scrupulous in an affair of such dignity,' said I.

'Well then,' said he, 'what do they mean by a Church being national or representative?

Surely they cannot mean that it must be an institution which everyone in the country approves of. There never has been or will be such a thing in this world. No one would dream of saying that the Government from time to time in office in this country was not both national and representative, although it is only approved of by a majority, and that perhaps a small majority of the people. Must they not mean by national—that which is approved of by the majority of the nation?'

'Certainly they must,' said I. 'But how are you to discover what proportion of the nation are adherents of any particular form of religious belief? For the opponents of the State Church have always stoutly refused to permit a religious census to be taken, and that would be the only reliable test.'

'I know,' said the stranger, 'that they show a little nervousness in this matter; and the absence of such a census does make the

inquiry difficult. But so far as there arc any
statistics to be obtained upon this question at
all, they all go to support what we should have
imagined *à priori* from the mere fact of the
existence of the Church—namely, that the
majority of the nation, and a large majority,
arc the adherents of this form of Christianity.
If we look at the returns[1] from the schools,
the cemeteries, the registers of marriages, the
army and navy, and the workhouses in this
country, where alone we have at the present
time an opportunity of obtaining statistics
upon this point, it is found that more than
72 per cent. of the total number of individuals
are members of the Established Church. And
when we consider that these statistics are
compiled for the most part from the lowest
stratum of society only, and the one in which

---

[1] See Report of *Education Dept.* 1871, c. 406; *Burials,*
Session 1860, Parl. Paper, 560; *Reg.-General's Report,* 1873;
Army, Parl. Paper, No. 170, Session 1871; *Navy,* do. No.
132, 1876; *Union Workhouses,* Paper No. 157, Session 1876.

the National Church has undeniably the fewest
adherents, we must be convinced, from this
calculation alone, that a large majority of the
nation approve of the Established Church.

'Thus, so far as we have any facts to
guide us, they disprove the assertions of our
antagonists. But may we not further say to
them this? If it is once admitted that it
is a good thing that some Christian Church
should be established in the country, it is
obvious that we must select one of the forms
of Christianity already existing for the purpose. In these days of multiplicity of sects,
it is impossible to find a Church which shall
represent all shades of religious belief. A
really Catholic religion is impossible, and so
we must be content with that which most
nearly approaches to it. Now, it could not be
pretended for a moment that any other sect
or form of Christianity now existing in this
country could by itself command a tithe of

the adherents which are numbered by our existing Church.'

' Certainly not,' said I.

'And, moreover,' said he, 'there is no other form of Christian worship which is so representative in the sense of containing within its walls so great a variety of religious opinion. The extreme members of our Church differ very little in their opinions from Presbyterians at the one end, and from Roman Catholics at the other.'

' There is no other existing Church or sect which is nearly so Catholic,' said I, ' in this sense.'

' Then our existing Church is both national and representative,' said he, ' in that it is approved by the nation at large, and that it represents the greatest variety of Christian belief.'

' It is,' said I.

' And, indeed,' said he, ' we might even carry the argument further and say that our existing Church is national in another sense, as being the direct lineal representative — the self-successor, as the Latins would call it—of the original Church first established in this country.'

'Certainly,' said I.

'And, as such, is the natural heir and representative of the Christianity of the nation.'

'Most assuredly,' I replied. 'There has been no breach in the continuity of its succession from the Saxon days.'

'So much, then, for our argument, O Politician,' said he. 'Now for our rebuke. May we not say to those who complain that it is unfair upon ministers of other denominations that any particular form of Christianity should be established as the State Church, "What is your grievance? Do the ministers of the State religion command a monopoly of doing good? Do they prevent you from preaching and teaching, or making others virtuous and happy?

And if not, what do you complain of? Must they not answer that their real grievance is a jealousy of the social advantages of their brethren of the English Church ?'

'They must,' said I.

'Then should we not reason sharply with such men,' said he, 'and say to them: Is not your aim professedly one with that of the National Church—to promote the general good of the citizens? And have we not shown that that good is best promoted by the maintenance of the existing Church? Put away from you, then, a contemptible jealousy of the worldly advantages of others. Are you not all casting out devils in the same name? Be assured that, if you succeed in destroying this Church, you will never be able to establish another. And so the nation will be losers and you no gainers. Will not this be a fitting reprimand to men who profess to be anxious for the welfare of the State, and yet postpone

its interests to their own love of dignity and
reward ? '

' Certainly, O Stranger,' I said.

' Shall we say, then,' said he, ' that we have
established this : that it is essential for the per-
manent development of religion in the State
that some representative Church should be
recognised and established by law as the embodiment of national religious feeling, and as
the means by which that feeling obtains utter-
ance ? '

' That we have proved,' said I.

' And this would be a good thing even if it
had to be created ? '

' Yes, O Stranger,' said I.

' And that still more is it true in a case
where an ancient, national and representative
Church already exists, carrying with it, by
force of long association, the reverence and
affection of many thousands of the citizens ? '

' It would be madness to destroy it,' said I.

When I had said this the stranger paused
awhile, as if to recover his breath, like an
athlete after a course—for, indeed, he had
become quite excited as his argument pro-
ceeded. So I chimed in, to give him a little
breathing time, and said :

' O Stranger, I find it very difficult myself
to suggest any answer to this part of your
argument, and so I must call in some enthusiastic allies to help me. You know that we
have some near neighbours and fellow-subjects
called the Irish, very warm-hearted people. I
believe that they gave the Government of this
country no little trouble in your day—if I
might guess at your date by your appearance.'

' I know them only too well,' said he.

' Well,' said I, ' I will summon them to my
aid, and they will come in a compact body, I
promise you, and will assert, as with one voice,
that there was once a State Church established
in Ireland, a fairly old institution, which never-

theless did not command the reverence and
affection of the Irish people ; but was hated by
all but a small minority of them with a deadly
hatred ; and that eventually this Church was
disestablished, and deprived of its pre-eminence.
And they will say, further, that since this has
taken place, not only the mass of the people
are more contented, owing to the removal of
a grievance, but that the adherents of the
Church that was formerly established are far
more active and enthusiastic in the cause of
religion than they were before. What answer
can you find to give to this formidable crew,
O Stranger ? '

'I am glad,' said he, smiling, 'that you
allowed me a little rest before encountering
these fresh enemies. For, from what I hear,
I shall require all my powers of " staying,"
as I believe you now say on the race-course,
if I am to avert defeat at their hands. However, I am not unprepared for them, for I

have—though, as you might say, "at a distance"—followed this controversy as to the
Irish Church with great interest. So far, O
Politician, from the history of the Irish Protestant Church being an argument against the
position that I have maintained, it is in reality
a strong illustration of the truth of it. ' Have
we not, above all things, laid stress upon the
necessity of such an institution as a Church
being the natural outgrowth of national feeling, because it is impossible to create national
sentiment artificially ? '

' We have,' said I.

'And we adduced it as a strong argument
in favour of our existing English Church that
it was a truly national Church in this sense :
that the reverence which attached to it was the
result of the spontaneous sentiment of generations of the citizens.'

' We did,' said I.

' Well,' said he, ' in the case of the Irish

Church, matters were quite different. It was never a National Church in any sense of the term, but was an exotic introduced with a complete hierarchical organisation against the will of the people, who were almost entirely devoted to another and hostile form of Christianity, and it was regarded by them as a badge of conquest, a yoke of servitude. Or we might go back to an illustration that we have used before, and say that the English Church is the natural heir of the Church originally established in the country when it first became Christian; that, although it differs now to a considerable extent in doctrine and practice from its original form, nevertheless the change has been a natural one, prepared for, long before it actually took place, by a quiet revolution in the religious opinions of the people. But the Irish Church, on the other hand, was an intruder and usurper, artificially thrust into a seat of honour from which the rightful owner had been dispossessed. The natural result of this is much the same as when a man, instead of leaving his property to his son, leaves it all to a stranger. When the latter comes to take possession he finds that his neighbours look very coldly upon him.'

'I quite understand your meaning,' I replied.

'Well, then,' said he, 'is it not true that the Irish Church, so far from being an instance against our position, is a strong illustration of its truth? Does it not exhibit unmistakeably the fact that national sentiment cannot be artificially created; and that, therefore, when you find an institution which is regarded by many with sentimental reverence, it is much too precious to be destroyed?'

. 'It does,' said I, 'most clearly.'

'And as for their second point,' said he, 'that the adherents of the Irish Protestant Church have been much more active and enthusiastic since it was disestablished, may we not say that that also does not in any way affect our argument? In the old days the ministers of the State Church in Ireland were scattered throughout the country, without any regard to the religious opinions of the population to which they were sent; and, consequently, in the majority of instances, they were like small garrisons in a hostile country, surrounded by deadly enemies, without either means of attack or prospect of relief. No wonder that when they were so scattered and outnumbered they were disheartened. But now that the Protestants have called in all their outlying garrisons and have limited the sphere of their operations to a district which it is possible for them to defend properly with their existing resources, they naturally have taken heart from mere sympathy and companionship, and are prepared to begin a new campaign with fresh vigour.'

'That is so,' I replied.

'In fact,' said he, 'in Ireland Protestants are only a sect, who were at one time artificially thrust into the position of a State Church, contrary to the will of the people, and have now returned to their natural position.'

'Undoubtedly,' said I.

'But their failure does not affect our Protestant Church in England,' said he, 'which . is natural and not artificial, supported by the nation and not detested, and is by far the most numerous and powerful of all the Christian communions in the country.'

'Now let us turn to our other opponents, O Politician,' said the stranger, 'those, I mean, who think that religion is a good thing, and that in some way an Established Church is a good thing, but who object to having, as they say, to submit their consciences and faith to secular control. And first let us say to them: Are you not mistaken, most worthy gentlemen, in saying this? Surely the State does not either prescribe or control the doctrines and practices of individuals. It defines and explains the doctrines and practices of the national Church, and it controls the persons who administer them. Let me illustrate my meaning familiarly, and do not laugh at me if I show a surprising ignorance of business ways, for in my day philosophers did not venture much into the city. But I fancy I was once told by some plump and substantial shades, who had lately left that great centre of commerce to join us in the other world, that in these days there are numerous associations for the sake of trade called Joint-stock Companies. That they are compelled by law to draw up and publish statutes which they call Articles of Association, by which the rights and liabilities of their members and officers are defined and controlled; so that, for instance, anyone by studying the articles of a company can inform himself at once of the exact limits of the directors' authority.

'Is that so, or were those business-like shades making fun of me?'

'You are correct,' said I.

'And further,' said he, 'that if any director exceeds the limits of his authority, he is liable for it to the uttermost farthing, and may be ejected from his office, and even imprisoned.'

'Certainly,' said I.

'And yet it is no hardship upon him,' continued the stranger, 'because he knew when he took upon himself the office of director exactly what his rights and liabilities would be, and he need not have accepted the post if he did not like the terms upon which it was held. But on the other hand it is essential to the security of the public that they should know the precise power and authority of anyone holding himself out as a director of a company.'

'You are quite an authority upon company law,' said I.

'Well then,' said he, smiling, 'if it is not impious to argue from the affairs of Mammon to those of God, may we not say that it is just the same with reference to the control that the State exercises over our national Church? It has certain formulæ drawn up by the Church and sanctioned by the State, which prescribe the doctrines and the practices which are to be observed and performed by those who hold themselves out to the public as the ministers of the State religion. They need not enter the orders of that Church unless they please, but if they do, and by so doing make themselves directors, so to speak, of the national Church, they must not exceed their power, or they will have to be ejected from the Church or otherwise punished. And there is no hardship in this, for they knew at the time when they took orders, both what doctrines and practices they would have to conform to, and what would be the consequence of nonconformity.'

'They did it with their eyes open,' said I.

'And, moreover,' said the stranger, 'it is very important that the public should be able to rely upon the ostensible ministers of the national Church remaining within the bounds to which they have agreed to conform.'

'They have a right to expect it,' said I.

'The State then only steps in,' 'said he, 'in the interests of the public, to prevent the agents of the Church from exceeding their authority; but it compels no person either to profess the doctrines of the Church or to remain within its walls against his will.'

'You have explained this very clearly,' said I; 'it is almost a pity that you are not a lawyer.'

'Oh,' said the stranger, laughing, 'I have had some little practice in that direction. But for these men who object to the State control of the Church: having hinted to them that their legal and logical ideas are not exact, let us apologise to them if we have wounded their feelings by such commonplace illustrations as we have used, and make a very humble petition to them and say, as we said to our other opponents : The interests of the State demand such a control. Will you not, then, either sacrifice your scruples to that interest or else leave our national Church altogether ?

'We must refer them back again to our show, and they will see there many scenes in which the absence of a State control over the Church has endangered the existence of the State. We will show them a time when the ministers of the Church professed obedience only to an authority resident in a foreign land. When that authority, having

absolute dominion over the convictions and
consciences of men, taught the citizens of this
land that their first duty was, not to the
country in which they lived, or to its Government and laws, but to the irresponsible commands of a foreign ecclesiastic. Nay, that
authority even ventured, on more than one
occasion, to proclaim to the citizens of this
country that their sovereign was a usurper;
that it was lawful for subjects to depose and
even kill their rulers for religious reasons—
and that even in the case of one of our
most wise and virtuous sovereigns. Can we
permit an irresponsible power independent of
the State Government, to wield so tremendous
an influence over our citizens, and that ostensibly in the guise of ministers or bishops of
our national Church ?'

'Certainly not,' said I. 'If this Church is
to be a national Church we cannot allow her
to turn traitor.'

'And we might also say, might we not?' said he, 'that this is a reason, why, if possible, a national Church should be a Protestant Church. Because a Roman Catholic Church can never be independent of foreign control, and consequently its interests must often conflict with those of our country. In short, it can never be truly national.'

'It cannot,' said I. 'We have only to look at the history of Europe to see that.'

'And as for those,' said he, 'who because of this State control or for other conscientious reasons cannot bring themselves to believe the doctrines of our Church as declared by the State authority: we would not have them voluntarily to act a lie, by pretending to conform to that which they do not believe, but we will only implore them, even if they cannot believe themselves, at all events not to prevent others from believing. I think they cannot fail to be convinced that both Christianity and the establishment of a national Christian Church is a good thing for the nation at large. And as they are for the most part philanthropical people, we will beg them not to destroy an institution which, whatever may be the theoretical premises upon which it depends, is of obvious practical benefit to mankind. For, indeed, even our bitterest opponents cannot say that its doctrines may not *possibly* be true, or that it is *impossible* their own theories may be false.'

'Certainly not,' said I.

'Then,' he continued, 'with such men the certainty of practical result should outweigh the doubtful issue of theoretical problems.'

I assented.

'And, indeed,' said the stranger, 'we might further remind those who cannot bring their consciences to believe in the doctrines of our national Church, that at least the establishment of such a Church is a great bulwark against intolerance and bigotry, both within and without its walls.

' For, O Politician, if a man can regard a great number of others, whose religious views differ very much from his own, as, nevertheless, members of the same Church as himself, and brethren with him in faith, must not that fact alone tend to make him more tolerant and larger hearted than if he were merely a member of a small isolated sect ? Besides, the fact that men differing widely in their interpretation of ceremonies and articles of faith can yet administer the same sacraments and use the same services, is in itself a Catholic element in our existing Church, which must produce greater tolerance amongst its members than can be found in any religious body whose doctrines and practices are rigid and uniform.

' Do you not think that if our existing national Church were disestablished and, thus

losing its bond of cohesion, were broken up, as
it infallibly would be, into a number of petty
sects, religious strife, bigotry and intolerance
would be far more general and bitter than
they now are? And that to the incalculable
harm and loss of the nation ; for while the
sheep-dogs are quarrelling the flock perish.'

'I am afraid that such would be the case,'
said I.

'Most men,' continued the stranger, 'are
naturally intolerant, and that very often in proportion to the strength of their convictions.
But yet words have a great power over them,
and they will tolerate the views of others who
professedly belong to their own communion,
although they would reprobate them in
strangers.

'And, again, there are some kind and
loving souls who long for peace, and who de-
light in the idea that in our Church men of
very different opinions can with one voice give

glory to God. Are we, then, to give a spur
to intolerance while we check the curb of
love ?'

'Not if we are skilful drivers,' said I.

'And, remember,' he continued, 'that the
same bigotry which will be exhibited between
the rival sects of Christianity will also be rife
between those who are Christians and those
who are not.

'The garment of our Church may be made
of various threads, but it is without seam—let
us not rend it.'

'It will be useless in pieces,' said I ; 'and
we have no similar material wherewith to
patch the rent.'

'Well, then,' added the stranger, 'what
more remains ? What further objections can
anyone offer to our national Church ? Have
we not disposed of all our adversaries ?'

'Not quite,' said I, 'for there yet remain
some persons, very precise gentlemen, who will

say that you are, upon your own confession, instructing the whole nation in a lie ; and that you must not do evil that good may come.'

'Oh,' said he, laughingly, 'I will put these puritanical gentlemen in a dilemma. Either Christianity is true, and therefore manifestly good : or it is false, and yet it is good.

'But let us first admit candidly,' said he, 'that if the rulers of the State were to undertake themselves to teach the citizens, as a vital and essential truth, a religious creed which they did not believe, they would in all probability fail. Because it is notorious that a man to be a successful teacher must himself believe in the principles which he teaches ; for otherwise he is half-hearted, and his disciples readily perceive it. But we do not suggest that the rulers should themselves inculcate these truths, but that they should merely give free scope to the exertions of those who believe them.

There are plenty of willing labourers for the harvest, and all that they ask is that they may not be impeded in their work. Leave us only our existing appliances, say they, and we will ask no more. Surely these are earnest men who believe in what they teach, and will convert the ignorant. Do not they deserve encouragement?'

'I think they do,' said I. 'In fact, they merely put in a plea for toleration.'

'Just so,' said he. 'And then, again, we must remind these opponents that, although we have been treating of this Christianity as though it were a "noble lie," still neither they nor anyone else has ever proved that it is so. Those philosophers who have most keenly criticised this religion can say no more than this: "It is not proved; therefore, we believe it to be false; but it may possibly be true."

'And, indeed, were it necessary for us to do

so, I would remind those who say that the
Divine origin of Christianity is not proved of
a very old story :

'Once, in the first beginnings of this faith,
there was a solemn council held by its enemies
to deliberate as to how they might put an
end to it. And one of the council, a doctor
learned in the law, rose up, and advised the
council not to interfere with it. " For," said
he, " all such devices, if they do not come from
God, will come to nought of themselves ; and
if this one does not come to nought of itself,
mayhap you may fight against God in trying to
suppress it."

'Nay, even one of their own modern philosophers[1] has said, not once, but many times
(for he is fond of repetition), that the only
way of knowing what is the will of God is
by considering what conduces to the greatest
happiness of the greatest number of mankind.

[1] Austin, *Jurisprudence.*

I

'Now, if we accept either of these tests, should we not have to admit that the strong probability seems to be that this religion comes of God?'

'It would seem so,' said I.

'But even if it is not true,' he continued, 'it is nevertheless good, in that it makes our citizens good.

'Do you ever remember to have heard the account of the death of a celebrated philosopher amongst the Greeks, who was condemned to death by his countrymen for teaching blasphemy about the gods?'

'I think I know the man you mean,' said I. 'It was Socrates the son of Sophroniscus.'

'Just so,' said he. 'Perhaps you may remember that when he addressed his fellow-citizens for the last time after they had condemned him to death,[1] he said that he forgave them their share in his death; for, indeed, it

---

[1] Plato, *Ap. Soc.* 40, 41.

would be more grievous to them than to him ;
that he had endeavoured all his life to be a
good man, and that it mattered not to a good
man what kind of existence he happened upon
after death. For that, in any case, his journey
to the next world would be no ill-faring.
Whether he should go to join the ghosts of
the departed in Hades, as their religion
taught, or whether death was but "a sleep
and a forgetting," a man who had lived a life
of self-denial and virtue upon earth would fare
well all the same. For if the account given by
their religion were true, the spirit of the good
man would fly off to join the ranks of the
heroes of old time, there to share in their
ineffable converse. Whereas, if death was but
a sleep, should we "dream perchance," the
dreams of the good man would be sweet and
his rest sound. So that, in any case, whatever
might be true of the life after death, it must
be all the better with a man hereafter for his

having been good and self-sacrificing in this life. That no real evil can happen to a good man in this life or in the next.

'Now let us apply this tale to our own case, O Politician ; and say to our opponents that our citizens will not know whether our Christianity is true or false, until after their death. So that, at all events, they will not be acting a conscious lie while they live. If Christianity turns out to be true after all, then their everlasting happiness will be secured if they have obeyed its precepts in this life ; but even if it turns out to be false, and life after death is something else from that which Christianity teaches, still, having been true followers of it during this life, and having been good and self-sacrificing, they will be a blessing to the State while they live, and when they die, whatever may be the condition in which they may find themselves, they may be confident that in no case can it be otherwise than well

with them. And, after all, the great object of
the politician is to find some power which
will make the citizens virtuous and self-sacrificing in this life.'

'Certainly,' said I.

'May we, then, conclude,' said he, 'that the
object of our vision is accomplished? That
you have found the power for which you have
sought so long? And that the arguments of its
adversaries have not prevailed against it?'

'We have,' said I; 'and I am entirely
satisfied with our conclusions.'

When I said this, the stranger smiled cheer-
fully, and stretched out his hand as if to bid
me farewell. But when his hand touched
mine, a sudden darkness and heaviness over-
came me, and I sank upon the ground in a
deep sleep. And when I awoke I found myself in the place where I was when the stranger
first accosted me; and he and all his show
had vanished away.

At first I could scarcely remember what had happened to me ; but as my faculties returned all that I had seen and heard rushed vividly upon my recollection. Though, even now, I seem to doubt whether I saw and heard in truth, or did but dream. But whether it was a waking or a sleeping vision, its lessons remain the same.

'And now,' said the politician to us all, ' I have detained you too long already ; and I, for one, shall be scolded if I remain away from home any longer.'

So saying, he bade us good-night, and departed ; and we shortly dispersed to our several homes, pondering deeply upon all these things.

Thus ends my tale. Let me briefly recapitulate the argument that I have outlined :—

(A.) That it is manifest from historical experience—

1. That disciplined religious enthusiasm is the great motive power which makes a nation successful ;

2. That the Christian religion is the great motive power that causes men to sacrifice themselves for the good of others, and thus makes a nation virtuous and happy.

(B.) That if this was not manifest from history, we should have expected it to be the case, *à priori*, from the known constitution of the human mind.

(C.) That, therefore, religion and, more especially, Christianity, is an important factor in politics, and at any rate cannot be ignored.

(D.) That the influence of Christianity is uniformly good, and that in the most important national and individual interests.

(E.) That it produces an effect for good which no legislation can produce, and that nothing but itself has ever been known to produce.

(F.) That, whether true or false, Christianity must do good and cannot do harm to anyone either in this world or the next.

(G.) That, therefore, the politician's duty, *whether he believes it to be true or false*, is to develop and utilise it.

(H.) That, assuming Christianity to be good for a nation, it is essential that it should be embodied in some definite national Church—

1. As a visible rallying-point and example for the national faith ;

2. As a means of national devotion ;

3. As a means of national control over a very formidable political power ;

4. As a bulwark against intolerance and bigotry.

(I.) That, this being so, if we did not find a Church established, it would be wise and statesmanlike, if possible, to create one.

(J.) That, *à fortiori*, it would be madness to destroy a Church already created, and which has been invested by the veneration of ages with a sentimental power over men's minds, which can never be replaced if once destroyed.

I have also endeavoured to suggest an answer to the various objections that are urged against the existing endowment and establishment of the Church.

They most of them stand or fall with the original position—namely, that the object at which the Church aims is one which is all-important for the welfare of the citizens.

If this is established, the argument drawn from the jealousies of other denominations is hardly deserving of a serious answer.

I have purposely avoided suggesting (except in one place, which does not affect the general argument) the truth of the doctrines upon which Christianity is based. But I hope I have, at all events, sufficiently indicated the effects of Christianity upon men's lives and conduct, as historical and psychological, and

not as theological, phenomena, to convince any
reasonable person that, whether it be true or
whether it be false, our national Church can
be shown to be based, as I said at the out-
set, upon a political expediency amounting to
a necessity.

The showman of my dialogue has probably been recognised by his well-known
aphorisms as Francis Bacon.

I chose him for the character because I
believe that the bitterness of the controversy
between religion and secularism is chiefly
owing to two causes :—

1. Want of definition of the object of the
inquiry ;

2. The neglect of historical investigation.

To call men's attention to these two
preliminaries of philosophical discussion was
Bacon's greatest achievement.

To anyone who looks back over the field
of time, and sees that almost all the most

vivid and dramatic incidents in the world's history, even in classical times, from the days of Polycrates of Samos, or Decius Mus and Curtius, down to our own, have been in some way connected with religious emotions, it may seem strange that in these days it should be the habit of a large class of controversialists to ignore religion as a political power altogether. Francis Bacon would have taught them better. He would have led them to look at the world's history, and from that record learn for themselves the lesson which he deduced, and which I have taken for my motto.

'The human intellect is not all of pure intelligence, but receives an infusion from the will and the emotions.'

LONDON : PRINTED BY
SPOTTISWOODE AND CO., NEW-STREET SQUARE
AND PARLIAMENT STREET

A LIST OF

C. KEGAN PAUL AND CO.'S

PUBLICATIONS.

7.81.

A LIST OF
C. KEGAN PAUL AND CO.'S
PUBLICATIONS.

ADAMS (F. O.), F.R.G.S.

The History of Japan. From the Earliest Period to the Present Time. New Edition, revised. 2 volumes. With Maps and Plans. Demy 8vo. Cloth, price 21s. each.

ADAMS (W. D.).

Lyrics of Love, from Shake- speare to Tennyson. Selected and arranged by. Fcap. 8vo. Cloth extra, gilt edges, price 3s. 6d.

ADAMSON (H. T.), B.D.

The Truth as it is in Jesus. Crown 8vo. Cloth, price 8s. 6d.

The Three Sevens. Crown 8vo. Cloth, price 5s. 6d.

A. K. H. B.

From a Quiet Place. A New Volume of Sermons. Crown 8vo. Cloth, price 5s.

ALBERT (Mary).

Holland and her Heroes to the year 1585. An Adaptation from Motley's "Rise of the Dutch Republic." Small crown 8vo. Cloth, price, 4s. 6d.

ALLEN (Rev. R.), M.A.

Abraham; his Life, Times, and Travels, 3,800 years ago. Second Edition. With Map. Post 8vo. Cloth, price 6s.

ALLEN (Grant), B.A.

Physiological Æsthetics. Large post 8vo. 9s.

ALLIES (T. W.), M.A.

Per Crucem ad Lucem. The Result of a Life. 2 vols. Demy 8vo. Cloth, price 25s.

A Life's Decision. Crown 8vo. Cloth, price 7s. 6d.

AMATEUR.

A Few Lyrics. Small crown 8vo. Cloth, price 2s.

ANDERSON (Col. R. P.).

Victories and Defeats. An Attempt to explain the Causes which have led to them. An Officer's Manual. Demy 8vo. Cloth, price 14s.

ANDERSON (R. C.), C.E.

Tables for Facilitating the Calculation of every Detail in connection with Earthen and Masonry Dams. Royal 8vo. Cloth, price £2 2s.

Antiope. A Tragedy. Large crown 8vo. Cloth, price 6s.

ARCHER (Thomas).

About my Father's Business. Work amidst the Sick, the Sad, and the Sorrowing. Crown 8vo. Cloth, price 2s. 6d.

ARMSTRONG (Richard A.), B.A.

Latter-Day Teachers. Six Lectures. Small crown 8vo. Cloth, price 2s. 6d.

Army of the North German Confederation.

A Brief Description of its Organization, of the Different Branches of the Service and their *rôle* in War, of its Mode of Fighting, &c. &c. Translated from the Corrected Edition, by permission of the Author, by Colonel Edward Newdigate. Demy 8vo. Cloth, price 5s.

ARNOLD (Arthur).

Social Politics. Demy 8vo. Cloth, price 14s.

Free Land. Crown 8vo. Cloth, price 6s.

AUBERTIN (J. J.).

Camoens' Lusiads. Portuguese Text, with Translation by. With Map and Portraits. 2 vols. Demy 8vo. Price 30s.

Seventy Sonnets of Camoens'. Portuguese text and translation, with some original poems. Dedicated to Captain Richard F. Burton. Printed on hand-made paper. Cloth, bevelled boards, gilt top, price 7s. 6d.

Aunt Mary's Bran Pie. By the author of "St. Olave's." Illustrated. Cloth, price 3s. 6d.

AVIA.

The Odyssey of Homer Done into English Verse. Fcap. 4to. Cloth, price 15s.

BADGER (George Perry), D.C.L.

An English-Arabic Lexicon. In which the equivalents for English words and idiomatic sentences are rendered into literary and colloquial Arabic. Royal 4to. Cloth, price £9 9s.

BAGEHOT (Walter).

Some Articles on the Depreciation of Silver, and Topics connected with it. Demy 8vo. Price 5s.

The English Constitution. A New Edition, Revised and Corrected, with an Introductory Dissertation on Recent Changes and Events. Crown 8vo. Cloth, price 7s. 6d.

Lombard Street. A Description of the Money Market. Seventh Edition. Crown 8vo. Cloth, price 7s. 6d.

BAGOT (Alan).

Accidents in Mines: their Causes and Prevention. Crown 8vo. Cloth, price 6s.

BAKER (Sir Sherston, Bart.).

Halleck's International Law; or Rules Regulating the Intercourse of States in Peace and War. A New Edition, Revised, with Notes and Cases. 2 vols. Demy 8vo. Cloth, price 38s.

BAKER (Sir Sherston, Bart.)— *continued.*

The Laws relating to Quarantine. Crown 8vo. Cloth, price 12s. 6d.

BALDWIN (Capt. J. H.), F.Z.S.

The Large and Small Game of Bengal and the North-Western Provinces of India. 4to. With numerous Illustrations. Second Edition. Cloth, price 21s.

BANKS (Mrs. G. L.).

God's Providence House. New Edition. Crown 8vo. Cloth, price 3s. 6d.

Ripples and Breakers. Poems. Square 8vo. Cloth, price 5s.

BARLEE (Ellen).

Locked Out: a Tale of the Strike. With a Frontispiece. Royal 16mo. Cloth, price 1s. 6d.

BARNES (William).

An Outline of English Speechcraft. Crown 8vo. Cloth, price 4s.

Poems of Rural Life, in the Dorset Dialect. New Edition, complete in 1 vol. Crown 8vo. Cloth, price 8s. 6d.

Outlines of Redecraft (Logic). With English Wording. Crown 8vo. Cloth, price 3s.

BARTLEY (George C. T.).

Domestic Economy: Thrift in Every Day Life. Taught in Dialogues suitable for Children of all ages. Small crown 8vo. Cloth, limp, 2s.

BAUR (Ferdinand), Dr. Ph.

A Philological Introduction to Greek and Latin for Students. Translated and adapted from the German of. By C. KEGAN PAUL, M.A. Oxon., and the Rev. E. D. STONE, M.A., late Fellow of King's College, Cambridge, and Assistant Master at Eton. Second and revised edition. Crown 8vo. Cloth, price 6s.

BAYNES (Rev. Canon R. H.).

At the Communion Time. A Manual for Holy Communion. With a preface by the Right Rev.

BAYNES (Rev. Canon R. H.)—*continued.*

the Lord Bishop of Derry and Raphoe. Cloth, price 1s. 6d.

  ** Can also be had bound in French morocco, price 2s. 6d.; Persian morocco, price 3s.; Calf, or Turkey morocco, price 3s. 6d.

BELLINGHAM (Henry), **Barrister-at-Law.**

Social Aspects of Catholicism and Protestantism in their Civil Bearing upon Nations. Translated and adapted from the French of M. le Baron de Haulleville. With a Preface by His Eminence Cardinal Manning. Second and cheaper edition. Crown 8vo. Cloth, price 3s. 6d.

BENNETT (Dr. W. C.).

Narrative Poems & Ballads. Fcap. 8vo. Sewed in Coloured Wrapper, price 1s.

Songs for Sailors. Dedicated by Special Request to H. R. H. the Duke of Edinburgh. With Steel Portrait and Illustrations. Crown 8vo. Cloth, price 3s. 6d.

  An Edition in Illustrated Paper Covers, price 1s.

Songs of a Song Writer. Crown 8vo. Cloth, price 6s.

BENT (J. Theodore).

Genoa. How the Republic Rose and Fell. With 18 Illustrations. Demy 8vo. Cloth, price 18s.

BETHAM - EDWARDS (Miss M.).

Kitty. With a Frontispiece. Crown 8vo. Cloth, price 6s.

BEVINGTON (L. S.).

Key Notes. Small crown 8vo. Cloth, price 5s.

Blue Roses; or, Helen Malinofska's Marriage. By the Author of "Véra." 2 vols. Fifth Edition. Cloth, gilt tops, 12s.

  ** Also a Cheaper Edition in 1 vol. With Frontispiece. Crown 8vo. Cloth, price 6s.

BLUME (Major W.).

The Operations of the German Armies in France, from Sedan to the end of the war of 1870-

BLUME (Major W.)—*continued.*

71. With Map. From the Journals of the Head-quarters Staff. Translated by the late E. M. Jones, Maj. 20th Foot, Prof. of Mil. Hist., Sandhurst. Demy 8vo. Cloth, price 9s.

BOGUSLAWSKI (Capt. A. von).

Tactical Deductions from the War of 1870-71. Translated by Colonel Sir Lumley Graham, Bart., late 18th (Royal Irish) Regiment. Third Edition, Revised and Corrected. Demy 8vo. Cloth, price 7s.

BONWICK (J.), **F.R.G.S.**

Egyptian Belief and Modern Thought. Large post 8vo. Cloth, price 10s. 6d.

Pyramid Facts and Fancies. Crown 8vo. Cloth, price 5s.

The Tasmanian Lily. With Frontispiece. Crown 8vo. Cloth, price 5s.

Mike Howe, the Bushranger of Van Diemen's Land. With Frontispiece. New and cheaper edition. Crown 8vo. Cloth, price 3s. 6d.

BOWEN (H. C.), **M. A.**

English Grammar for Beginners. Fcap. 8vo. Cloth, price 1s.

Studies in English, for the use of Modern Schools. Small crown 8vo. Cloth, price 1s. 6d.

Simple English Poems. English Literature for Junior Classes. In Four Parts. Parts I. and II., price 6d. each, now ready.

BOWRING (Sir John).

Autobiographical Recollections. With Memoir by Lewin B. Bowring. Demy 8vo. Price 14s.

Brave Men's Footsteps. By the Editor of "Men who have Risen." A Book of Example and Anecdote for Young People. With Four Illustrations by C. Doyle. Sixth Edition. Crown 8vo. Cloth, price 3s. 6d.

BRIALMONT (Col. A.).

Hasty Intrenchments. Translated by Lieut. Charles A. Empson, R.A. With Nine Plates. Demy 8vo. Cloth, price 6s.

BRIDGETT (Rev. J. E.).
History of the Holy Eucha-
rist in Great Britain. 2 vols.,
demy 8vo. Cloth, price 18s.

BRODRICK (The Hon. G. C.).
Political Studies. Demy
8vo. Cloth, price 14s.

BROOKE (Rev. S. A.), M. A.
The Late Rev. F. W. Ro-
bertson, M.A., Life and Letters
of. Edited by.
  I. Uniform with the Sermons.
2 vols. With Steel Portrait. Price
7s. 6d.
  II. Library Edition. 8vo. With
Portrait. Price 12s.
  III. A Popular Edition, in 1 vol.
8vo. Price 6s.
The Spirit of the Christian
Life. A New Volume of Sermons.
Crown 8vo. Cloth, price 7s. 6d.
Theology in the English
Poets. — COWPER, COLERIDGE,
WORDSWORTH, and BURNS. Fourth
and Cheaper Edition. Post 8vo.
Cloth, price 5s.
Christ in Modern Life.
Fifteenth and Cheaper Edition.
Crown 8vo. Cloth, price 5s.
Sermons. First Series.
Eleventh Edition. Crown 8vo. Cloth,
price 6s.
Sermons. Second Series.
Fourth Edition. Crown 8vo. Cloth,
price 7s.
The Fight of Faith. Ser-
mons preached on various occasions.
Fifth Edition. Crown 8vo. Cloth,
price 7s. 6d.

BROOKE (W. G.), M. A.
The Public Worship
Regulation Act. With a Classified
Statement of its Provisions, Notes,
and Index. Third Edition, Revised
and Corrected. Crown 8vo. Cloth,
price 3s. 6d.
Six Privy Council Judg-
ments—1850-1872. Annotated by.
Third Edition. Crown 8vo. Cloth,
price 9s.

BROUN (J. A.).
Magnetic Observations at
Trevandrum and Augustia
Malley. Vol. I. 4to. Cloth,
price 63s.
  The Report from above, separately
sewed, price 21s.

BROWN (Rev. J. Baldwin).
The Higher Life. Its Reality,
Experience, and Destiny. Fifth and
Cheaper Edition. Crown 8vo. Cloth,
price 5s.
Doctrine of Annihilation
in the Light of the Gospel
of Love. Five Discourses. Third
Edition. Crown 8vo. Cloth, price
2s. 6d.
The Christian Policy of
Life. A Book for Young Men of
Business. New and Cheaper Edition.
Crown 8vo. Cloth, price 3s. 6d.

BROWN (J. Croumbie), LL.D.
Reboisement in France; or,
Records of the Replanting of the
Alps, the Cevennes, and the Pyre-
nees with Trees, Herbage, and Bush.
Demy 8vo. Cloth, price 12s. 6d.
The Hydrology of Southern
Africa. Demy 8vo. Cloth, price
10s. 6d.

BROWNE (W. R.).
The Inspiration of the
New Testament. With a Preface
by the Rev. J. P. NORRIS, D.D.
Fcap. 8vo. Cloth, price 2s. 6d.

BRYANT (W. C.)
Poems. Red-line Edition.
With 24 Illustrations and Portrait of
the Author. Crown 8vo. Cloth extra,
price 7s. 6d.
  A Cheaper Edition, with Frontispiece. Small crown 8vo. Cloth, price
3s. 6d.

BURCKHARDT (Jacob).
The Civilization of the Pe-
riod of the Renaissance in Italy.
Authorized translation, by S. G. C.
Middlemore. 2 vols. Demy 8vo.
Cloth, price 24s.

BURTON (Mrs. Richard).
The Inner Life of Syria,
Palestine, and the Holy Land.
With Maps, Photographs, and
Coloured Plates. 2 vols. Second
Edition. Demy 8vo. Cloth, price 24s.
  . Also a Cheaper Edition in
one volume. Large post 8vo. Cloth,
price 10s. 6d.

BURTON (Capt. Richard F.).
The Gold Mines of Midian
and the Ruined Midianite
Cities. A Fortnight's Tour in

BURTON (Capt. Richard F.)— *continued.*

North Western Arabia. With numerous Illustrations. Second Edition. Demy 8vo. Cloth, price 18s.

The Land of Midian Revisited. With numerous illustrations on wood and by Chromolithography. 2 vols. Demy 8vo. Cloth, price 32s.

BUSBECQ (Ogier Ghiselin de).
His Life and Letters. By Charles Thornton Forster, M.D. and F. H. Blackburne Daniell, M.D. 2 vols. With Frontispieces. Demy 8vo. Cloth, price 24s.

BUTLER (Alfred J.).
Amaranth and Asphodel. Songs from the Greek Anthology.— I. Songs of the Love of Women. II. Songs of the Love of Nature. III. Songs of Death. IV. Songs of Hereafter. Small crown 8vo. Cloth, price 2s.

BYRNNE (E. Fairfax).
Milicent. A Poem. Small crown 8vo. Cloth, price 6s.

CALDERON.
Calderon's Dramas: The Wonder-Working Magician—Life is a Dream—The Purgatory of St. Patrick. Translated by Denis Florence MacCarthy. Post 8vo. Cloth, price 10s.

CANDLER (H.).
The Groundwork of Belief. Crown 8vo. Cloth, price 7s.

CARPENTER (W. B.), M.D.
The Principles of Mental Physiology. With their Applications to the Training and Discipline of the Mind, and the Study of its Morbid Conditions. Illustrated. Fifth Edition. 8vo. Cloth, price 12s.

CARPENTER (Dr. Philip P.).
His Life and Work. Edited by his brother, Russell Lant Carpenter. With portrait and vignette. Second Edition. Crown 8vo. Cloth, price 7s. 6d.

CAVALRY OFFICER.
Notes on Cavalry Tactics, Organization, &c. With Diagrams Demy 8vo. Cloth, price 12s.

CERVANTES.
The Ingenious Knight Don Quixote de la Mancha. A New Translation from the Originals of 1605 and 1608. By A. J. Duffield. With Notes. 3 vols. demy 8vo. Cloth, price 42s.

CHAPMAN (Hon. Mrs. E. W.).
A Constant Heart. A Story. 2 vols. Cloth, gilt tops, price 12s.

CHEYNE (Rev. T. K.).
The Prophecies of Isaiah. Translated, with Critical Notes and Dissertations by. Two vols., demy 8vo. Cloth, price 25s.

Children's Toys, and some Elementary Lessons in General Knowledge which they teach. Illustrated. Crown 8vo. Cloth, price 5s.

Clairaut's   **Elements**   of Geometry. Translated by Dr. Kaines, with 145 figures. Crown 8vo. Cloth, price 4s. 6d.

CLARKE (Mary Cowden).
Honey from the Weed. Crown 8vo. Cloth, price 7s.

CLAYDEN (P. W.).
England under Lord Beaconsfield. The Political History of the Last Six Years, from the end of 1873 to the beginning of 1880. Second Edition. With Index, and Continuation to March, 1880. Demy 8vo. Cloth, price 16s.

CLERY (C.), Lieut.-Col.
Minor Tactics. With 26 Maps and Plans. Fifth and Revised Edition. Demy 8vo. Cloth, price 16s.

CLODD (Edward), F.R.A.S.
The   **Childhood**   **of**   **the** World : a Simple Account of Man in Early Times. Sixth Edition. Crown 8vo. Cloth, price 3s.
A Special Edition for Schools. Price 1s.

The Childhood of Religions. Including a Simple Account of the Birth and Growth of Myths and Legends. Third Thousand. Crown 8vo. Cloth, price 5s.
A Special Edition for Schools Price 1s. 6d.

CLODD (Edward), F.R.A.S.—
continued.
Jesus of Nazareth. With a brief Sketch of Jewish History to the Time of His Birth. Small crown 8vo. Cloth, price 6s.

COGHLAN (J. Cole), D.D.
The Modern Pharisee and other Sermons. Edited by the Very Rev. A. H. Dickinson, D.D., Dean of Chapel Royal, Dublin. New and cheaper edition. Crown 8vo. Cloth, price 7s. 6d.

COLERIDGE (Sara).
Pretty Lessons in Verse for Good Children, with some Lessons in Latin, in Easy Rhyme. A New Edition. Illustrated. Fcap. 8vo. Cloth, price 3s. 6d.

Phantasmion. A Fairy Tale. With an Introductory Preface by the Right Hon. Lord Coleridge, of Ottery St. Mary. A New Edition. Illustrated. Crown 8vo. Cloth, price 7s. 6d.

Memoir and Letters of Sara Coleridge. Edited by her Daughter. Cheap Edition. With one Portrait. Cloth, price 7s. 6d.

COLLINS (Mortimer).
The Secret of Long Life. Small crown 8vo. Cloth, price 3s. 6d.
Inn of Strange Meetings, and other Poems. Crown 8vo. Cloth, price 5s.

COLOMB (Colonel).
The Cardinal Archbishop. A Spanish Legend in twenty-nine Cancions. Small crown 8vo. Cloth, price 5s.

CONNELL (A. K.).
Discontent and Danger in India. Small crown 8vo. Cloth, price 3s. 6d.

CONWAY (Hugh).
A Life's Idylls. Small crown 8vo. Cloth, price 3s. 6d.

COOKE (Prof. J. P.)
Scientific Culture. Crown 8vo. Cloth, price 1s.

COOPER (H. J.).
The Art of Furnishing on Rational and Æsthetic Principles. New and Cheaper Edition. Fcap. 8vo. Cloth, price 1s. 6d.

COPPÉE (François).
L'Exilée. Done into English Verse with the sanction of the Author by I. O. L. Crown 8vo. Vellum, price 5s.

CORFIELD (Prof.), M.D.
Health. Crown 8vo. Cloth, price 6s.

CORY (William).
A Guide to Modern Eng-lish History. Part I. MDCCCXV. —MDCCCXXX. Demy 8vo. Cloth, price 9s.

COURTNEY (W. L).
The Metaphysics of John Stuart Mill. Crown 8vo. Cloth, price 5s. 6d.

COWAN (Rev. William).
Poems : Chiefly Sacred, including Translations from some Ancient Latin Hymns. Fcap. 8vo. Cloth, price 5s.

COX (Rev. Sir G. W.), Bart.
A History of Greece from the Earliest Period to the end of the Persian War. New Edition. 2 vols. Demy 8vo. Cloth, price 36s.

The Mythology of the Aryan Nations. New Edition. 2 vols. Demy 8vo. Cloth, price 28s.

A General History of Greece from the Earliest Period to the Death of Alexander the Great, with a sketch of the subsequent History to the present time. New Edition. Crown 8vo. Cloth, price 7s. 6d.

Tales of Ancient Greece. New Edition. Small crown 8vo Cloth, price 6s.

School History of Greece. With Maps. New Edition. Fcap 8vo. Cloth, price 3s. 6d.

The Great Persian War from the Histories of Herodotus. New Edition. Fcap. 8vo. Cloth, price 3s. 6d.

A Manual of Mythology in the form of Question and Answer New Edition. Fcap. 8vo. Cloth, price 3s.

An Introduction to the Science of Comparative Mythology and Folk-Lore. Large crown 8vo. Cloth, price 9s.

COX (Rev. Sir G. W.), Bart., M.A., and EUSTACE HINTON JONES.

Popular Romances of the Middle Ages. Second Edition in one volume. Crown 8vo. Cloth, price 6s.

COX (Rev. Samuel).

A Commentary on the Book of Job. With a Translation. Demy 8vo. Cloth, price 15s.

Salvator Mundi; or, Is Christ the Saviour of all Men? Sixth Edition. Crown 8vo. Cloth, price 5s.

The Genesis of Evil, and other Sermons, mainly Expository. Second Edition. Crown 8vo. Cloth, price 6s.

CRAUFURD (A. H.).

Seeking for Light : Sermons. Crown 8vo. Cloth, price 5s.

CRAVEN (Mrs.).

A Year's Meditations. Crown 8vo. Cloth, price 6s.

CRAWFURD (Oswald).

Portugal, Old and New. With Illustrations and Maps. Demy 8vo. Cloth, price 16s.

CRESSWELL (Mrs. G.).

The King's Banner. Drama in Four Acts. Five Illustrations. 4to. Cloth, price 10s. 6d.

CROZIER (John Beattie), M.B.

The Religion of the Future. Crown 8vo. Cloth, price 6s.

DALTON (John Neale), M.A., R.N.

Sermons to Naval Cadets. Preached on board H.M.S. "Britannia." Second Edition. Small crown 8vo. Cloth, price 3s. 6d.

D'ANVERS (N. R.).

Parted. A Tale of Clouds and Sunshine. With 4 Illustrations. Extra Fcap. 8vo. Cloth, price 3s. 6d.

Little Minnie's Troubles. An Every-day Chronicle. With Four Illustrations by W. H. Hughes. Fcap. Cloth, price 3s. 6d.

D'ANVERS (N. R)—*continued.*

Pixie's Adventures ; or, the Tale of a Terrier. With 21 Illustrations. 16mo. Cloth, price 4s. 6d.

Nanny's Adventures; or, the Tale of a Goat. With 12 Illustrations. 16mo. Cloth, price 4s. 6d.

DAVIDSON (Rev. Samuel), D.D., LL.D.

The New Testament, trans-lated from the Latest Greek Text of Tischendorf. A New and thoroughly Revised Edition. Post 8vo. Cloth, price 10s. 6d.

Canon of the Bible : Its Formation, History, and Fluctuations. Third Edition, revised and enlarged. Small crown 8vo. Cloth, price 5s.

DAVIES (G. Christopher).

Rambles and Adventures of Our School Field Club. With Four Illustrations. Crown 8vo. Cloth, price 5s.

DAVIES (Rev. J. L.), M.A.

Theology and Morality. Essays on Questions of Belief and Practice. Crown 8vo. Cloth, price 7s. 6d.

DAVIES (T. Hart.).

Catullus. Translated into English Verse. Crown 8vo. Cloth, price 6s.

DAWSON (George), M.A.

Prayers, with a Discourse on Prayer. Edited by his Wife. Fifth Edition. Crown 8vo. Price 6s.

Sermons on Disputed Points and Special Occasions. Edited by his Wife. Third Edition. Crown 8vo. Cloth, price 6s.

Sermons on Daily Life and Duty. Edited by his Wife. Second Edition. Crown 8vo. Cloth, price 6s.

DE L'HOSTE (Col. E. P.).

The Desert Pastor, Jean Jarousseau. Translated from the French of Eugène Pelletan. With a Frontispiece. New Edition. Fcap. 8vo. Cloth, price 3s. 6d.

DE REDCLIFFE (Viscount Stratford), P.C., K.G., G.C.B.
Why am I a Christian?
Fifth Edition. Crown 8vo. Cloth, price 3s.

DESPREZ (Philip S.).
Daniel and John; or, the Apocalypse of the Old and that of the New Testament. Demy 8vo. Cloth, price 12s.

DE TOCQUEVILLE (A.).
Correspondence and Conversations of, with Nassau William Senior, from 1834 to 1859. Edited by M. C. M. Simpson. 2 vols. Post 8vo. Cloth, price 21s.

DE VERE (Aubrey).
Legends of the Saxon Saints. Small crown 8vo. Cloth, price 6s.

Alexander the Great. A Dramatic Poem. Small crown 8vo. Cloth, price 5s.

The Infant Bridal, and other Poems. A New and Enlarged Edition. Fcap. 8vo. Cloth, price 7s. 6d.

The Legends of St. Patrick, and other Poems. Small crown 8vo. Cloth, price 5s.

St. Thomas of Canterbury. A Dramatic Poem. Large fcap. 8vo. Cloth, price 5s.

Antar and Zara : an Eastern Romance. INISFAIL, and other Poems, Meditative and Lyrical. Fcap. 8vo. Price 6s.

The Fall of Rora, the Search after Proserpine, and other Poems, Meditative and Lyrical. Fcap. 8vo. Price 6s.

DOBELL (Mrs. Horace).
Ethelstone, Eveline, and other Poems. Crown 8vo. Cloth, price 6s.

DOBSON (Austin).
Vignettes in Rhyme and Vers de Société. Third Edition. Fcap. 8vo. Cloth, price 5s.

Proverbs in Porcelain. By the Author of "Vignettes in Rhyme." Second Edition. Crown 8vo. 6s.

Dorothy. A Country Story in Elegiac Verse. With Preface. Demy 8vo. Cloth, price 5s.

DOWDEN (Edward), LL.D.
Shakspere: a Critical Study of his Mind and Art. Fifth Edition. Large post 8vo. Cloth, price 12s.

Studies in Literature, 1789-1877. Large post 8vo. Cloth, price 12s.

Poems. Second Edition. Fcap. 8vo. Cloth, price 5s.

DOWNTON (Rev. H.), M.A.
Hymns and Verses. Original and Translated. Small crown 8vo. Cloth, price 3s. 6d.

DREWRY (G. O.), M.D.
The Common-Sense Management of the Stomach. Fifth Edition. Fcap. 8vo. Cloth, price 2s. 6d.

DREWRY (G. O.), M.D., and BARTLETT (H. C.), Ph.D., F.C.S.
Cup and Platter: or, Notes on Food and its Effects. New and cheaper Edition. Small 8vo. Cloth, price 1s. 6d.

DRUMMOND (Miss).
Tripps Buildings. A Study from Life, with Frontispiece. Small crown 8vo. Cloth, price 3s. 6d.

DUFFIELD (A. J.).
Don Quixote. His Critics and Commentators. With a Brief Account of the Minor Works of Miguel de Cervantes Saavedra, and a statement of the end and aim of the greatest of them all. A Handy Book for General Readers. Crown 8vo. Cloth, price 3s. 6d.

DU MONCEL (Count).
The Telephone, the Microphone, and the Phonograph. With 74 Illustrations. Small crown 8vo. Cloth, price 5s.

DUTT (Toru).
A Sheaf Gleaned in French Fields. New Edition, with Portrait. Demy 8vo. Cloth, price 10s. 6d.

A 2

DU VERNOIS (Col. von Verdy).

Studies in leading Troops.
An authorized and accurate Translation by Lieutenant H. J. T. Hildyard, 71st Foot. Parts I. and II. Demy 8vo. Cloth, price 7s.

EDEN (Frederick).

The Nile without a Dragoman. Second Edition. Crown 8vo. Cloth, price 7s. 6d.

EDGEWORTH (F. Y.).

Mathematical Psychics: an Essay on the Application of Mathematics to Social Science. Demy 8vo. Cloth, price 7s. 6d.

EDIS (Robert W.).

Decoration and Furniture of Town Houses. A series of Cantor Lectures delivered before the Society of Arts, 1880. Amplified and enlarged, with 29 full-page Illustrations and numerous sketches. Second Edition. Square 8vo. Cloth, price 12s. 6d.

EDMONDS (Herbert).

Well Spent Lives : a Series of Modern Biographies. Crown 8vo Price 5s.

Educational Code of the Prussian Nation, in its Present Form. In accordance with the Decisions of the Common Provincial Law, and with those of Recent Legislation. Crown 8vo. Cloth, price 2s. 6d.

EDWARDS (Rev. Basil).

Minor Chords; or, Songs for the Suffering: a Volume of Verse. Fcap. 8vo. Cloth, price 3s. 6d. ; paper, price 2s. 6d.

ELLIOT (Lady Charlotte).

Medusa and other Poems.
Crown 8vo. Cloth, price 6s.

ELLIOTT (Ebenezer), The Corn-Law Rhymer.

Poems. Edited by his Son, the Rev. Edwin Elliott, of St. John's, Antigua. 2 vols. Crown 8vo. Cloth, price 18s.

ELSDALE (Henry).

Studies in Tennyson's Idylls. Crown 8vo. Cloth, price 5s.

ELYOT (Sir Thomas).

The Boke named the Gouernour. Edited from the First Edition of 1531 by Henry Herbert Stephen Croft, M.A., Barrister-at-Law. With Portraits of Sir Thomas and Lady Elyot, copied by permission of her Majesty from Holbein's Original Drawings at Windsor Castle. 2 vols. fcap. 4to. Cloth, price 50s.

Epic of Hades (The).
By the author of " Songs of Two Worlds." Twelfth Edition. Fcap. 8vo. Cloth, price 7s. 6d.
* Also an Illustrated Edition with seventeen full-page designs in photomezzotint by GEORGE R. CHAPMAN. 4to. Cloth, extra gilt leaves, price 25s, and a Large Paper Edition, with portrait, price 10s. 6d.

EVANS (Anne).

Poems and Music. With Memorial Preface by Ann Thackeray Ritchie. Large crown 8vo. Cloth, price 7s. 6d.

EVANS (Mark).

The Gospel of Home Life.
Crown 8vo. Cloth, price 4s. 6d.

The Story of our Father's Love, told to Children. Fourth and Cheaper Edition. With Four Illustrations. Fcap. 8vo. Cloth, price 1s. 6d.

A Book of Common Prayer and Worship for Household Use, compiled exclusively from the Holy Scriptures. New and Cheaper Edition. Fcap. 8vo. Cloth, price 1s.

The King's Story Book.
In three parts. Fcap. 8vo. Cloth, price 1s. 6d. each.
** Parts I. and II., with eight illustrations and two Picture Maps, now ready.

EX-CIVILIAN.

Life in the Mofussil; or, Civilian Life in Lower Bengal. 2 vols. Large post 8vo. Price 14s.

FARQUHARSON (M.).

I. Elsie Dinsmore. Crown 8vo. Cloth, price 3s. 6d.

FARQUHARSON (M.)—*continued.*

II. **Elsie's Girlhood.** Crown 8vo. Cloth, price 3s. 6d.

III. **Elsie's Holidays at Roselands.** Crown 8vo. Cloth, price 3s. 6d.

FELKIN (H. M.).
Technical Education in a Saxon Town. Published for the City and Guilds of London Institute for the Advancement of Technical Education. Demy 8vo. Cloth, price 2s.

FIELD (Horace), B.A. Lond.
The Ultimate Triumph of Christianity. Small crown 8vo. Cloth, price 3s. 6d.

FINN (the late James), M.R.A.S.
Stirring Times ; or, Records from Jerusalem Consular Chronicles of 1853 to 1856. Edited and Compiled by his Widow. With a Preface by the Viscountess STRANGFORD. 2 vols. Demy 8vo. Price 30s.

FLOREDICE (W. H.).
A Month among the Mere Irish. Small crown 8vo. Cloth, price 5s.

Folkestone Ritual Case (The). The Argument, Proceedings Judgment, and Report, revised by the several Counsel engaged. Demy 8vo. Cloth, price 25s.

FORMBY (Rev. Henry).
Ancient Rome and its Connection with the Christian Religion : an Outline of the History of the City from its First Foundation down to the Erection of the Chair of St. Peter, A.D. 42-47. With numerous Illustrations of Ancient Monuments, Sculpture, and Coinage, and of the Antiquities of the Christian Catacombs. Royal 4to. Cloth extra, price 50s. Roxburgh, half-morocco, price 52s. 6d.

FOWLE (Rev. T. W.), M.A.
The Reconciliation of Religion and Science. Being Essays on Immortality, Inspiration, Miracles, and the Being of Christ. Demy 8vo. Cloth, price 10s. 6d.

The Divine Legation of Christ. Crown 8vo. Cloth, price 7s.

FRASER (Donald).
Exchange Tables of Sterling and Indian Rupee Currency, upon a new and extended system, embracing Values from One Farthing to One Hundred Thousand Pounds, and at Rates progressing, in Sixteenths of a Penny, from 1s. 9d. to 2s. 3d. per Rupee. Royal 8vo. Cloth, price 10s. 6d.

FRISWELL (J. Hain).
The Better Self. Essays for Home Life. Crown 8vo. Cloth, price 6s.

One of Two ; or, A Left-Handed Bride. With a Frontispiece. Crown 8vo. Cloth, price 3s. 6d.

GARDINER (Samuel R.) and J. BASS MULLINGER, M.A.
Introduction to the Study of English History. Large crown 8vo. Cloth, price 9s.

GARDNER (J.), M.D.
Longevity : The Means of Prolonging Life after Middle Age. Fourth Edition, Revised and Enlarged. Small crown 8vo. Cloth, price 4s.

GARRETT (E.).
By Still Waters. A Story for Quiet Hours. With Seven Illustrations. Crown 8vo. Cloth, price 6s.

GEBLER (Karl Von).
Galileo Galilei and the Roman Curia, from Authentic Sources. Translated with the sanction of the Author, by Mrs. GEORGE STURGE. Demy 8vo. Cloth, price 12s.

GEDDES (James).
History of the Administration of John de Witt, Grand Pensionary of Holland. Vol. I. 1623—1654. Demy 8vo., with Portrait. Cloth, price 15s.

GEORGE (Henry).
Progress and Poveity. An Inquiry into the Cause of Industrial Depressions and of Increase of Want with Increase of Wealth. The Remedy. Post 8vo. Cloth, price 7s. 6d.

GILBERT (Mrs.).
Autobiography and other Memorials. Edited by Josiah

GILBERT (Mrs.)—*continued*.
Gilbert. Third Edition. With Por
trait and several Wood Engravings.
Crown 8vo. Cloth, price 7s. 6d.

GLOVER (F.), M.A.
Exempla Latina. A First
Construing Book with Short Notes,
Lexicon, and an Introduction to the
Analysis of Sentences. Fcap. 8vo.
Cloth, price 2s.

GODWIN (William).
William Godwin: His
Friends and Contemporaries.
With Portraits and Facsimiles of the
handwriting of Godwin and his Wife.
By C. Kegan Paul. 2 vols. Demy
8vo. Cloth, price 28s.

The Genius of Christianity
Unveiled. Being Essays never
before published. Edited, with a
Preface, by C. Kegan Paul. Crown
8vo. Cloth, price 7s. 6d.

GOETZE (Capt. A. von).
Operations of the German
Engineers during the War of
1870-1871. Published by Authority,
and in accordance with Official Docu-
ments. Translated from the German
by Colonel G. Graham, V.C., C.B.,
R.E. With 6 large Maps. Demy
8vo. Cloth, price 21s.

GOLDSMID (Sir Francis Henry).
Memoir of. With Portrait.
Crown 8vo. Cloth, price 5s.

GOODENOUGH (Commodore J.
G.), R.N., C.B., C.M.G.
Memoir of, with Extracts from
his Letters and Journals. Edited by
his Widow. With Steel Engraved
Portrait. Square 8vo. Cloth, 5s.
*** Also a Library Edition with
Maps, Woodcuts, and Steel En-
graved Portrait. Square post 8vo.
Cloth, price 14s.

GOSSE (Edmund W.).
Studies in the Literature of
Northern Europe. With a Frontis-
piece designed and etched by Alma
Tadema. Large post 8vo. Cloth,
price 12s.

New Poems. Crown 8vo.
Cloth, price 7s. 6d.

GOULD (Rev. S. Baring), M.A.
Germany, Present and Past.
2 Vols. Demy 8vo. Cloth, price 21s.
The Vicar of Morwenstow:
a Memoir of the Rev. R. S. Hawker.
With Portrait. Third Edition, revised. Square post 8vo. Cloth, 10s. 6d.

GRAHAM (William), M.A.
The Creed of Science : Religious, Moral, and Social. Demy
8vo. Cloth, price 12s.

GREENOUGH (Mrs. Richard).
Mary Magdalene : A Poem.
Large post 8vo. Parchment antique,
price 6s.

GRIFFITH (Thomas), A.M.
The Gospel of the Divine
Life. A Study of the Fourth Evan-
gelist. Demy 8vo. Cloth, price 14s.

GRIMLEY (Rev. H. N.), M.A.
Tremadoc Sermons, chiefly
on the SPIRITUAL BODY, the UNSEEN
WORLD, and the DIVINE HUMANITY.
Second Edition. Crown 8vo. Cloth,
price 6s.

GRÜNER (M. L.).
Studies of Blast Furnace
Phenomena. Translated by L. D.
B. Gordon, F.R.S.E., F.G.S. Demy
8vo. Cloth, price 7s. 6d.

GURNEY (Rev. Archer).
Words of Faith and Cheer.
A Mission of Instruction and Sugges-
tion. Crown 8vo. Cloth, price 6s.

Gwen : A Drama in Mono-
logue. By the Author of the "Epic
of Hades." Second Edition. Fcap.
8vo. Cloth, price 5s.

HAECKEL (Prof. Ernst).
The History of Creation.
Translation revised by Professor E.
Ray Lankester, M.A., F.R.S. With
Coloured Plates and Genealogical
Trees of the various groups of both
plants and animals. 2 vols. Second
Edition. Post 8vo. Cloth, price 32s.

The History of the Evolu-
tion of Man. With numerous Illustrations. 2 vols. Large post 8vo.
Cloth, price 32s.

Freedom in Science and
Teaching. From the German of

HAECKEL (Prof. Ernst) — *continued.*

Ernst Haeckel, with a Prefatory Note by T. H. Huxley, F.R.S. Crown 8vo. Cloth, price 5*s.*

HALF-CROWN SERIES.

Sister Dora: a Biography. By Margaret Lonsdale.

True Words for Brave Men. A Book for Soldiers and Sailors. By the late Charles Kingsley.

An Inland Voyage. By R. L. Stevenson.

Travels with a Donkey. By R. L. Stevenson.

A Nook in the Apennines. By Leader Scott.

Notes of Travel. Being Extracts from the Journals of Count Von Moltke.

Letters from Russia. By Count Von Moltke.

English Sonnets. Collected and Arranged by J. Dennis.

Lyrics of Love from Shakespeare to Tennyson. Selected and Arranged by W. D. Adams.

London Lyrics. By Frederick Locker.

Home Songs for Quiet Hours. By the Rev. Canon R. H. Baynes.

Halleck's International Law; or, Rules Regulating the Intercourse of States in Peace and War. A New Edition, revised, with Notes and Cases. By Sir Sherston Baker, Bart. 2 vols. Demy 8vo. Cloth, price 38*s.*

HARDY (Thomas).

A Pair of Blue Eyes. New Edition. With Frontispiece. Crown 8vo. Cloth, price 6*s.*

The Return of the Native. New Edition. With Frontispiece. Crown 8vo. Cloth, price 6*s.*

HARRISON (Lieut.-Col. R.).

The Officer's Memorandum Book for Peace and War. Third Edition. Oblong 32mo. roan, with pencil, price 3*s. 6d.*

HARTINGTON (The Right Hon. the Marquis of), M.P.

Election Speeches in 1879 and 1880. With Address to the Electors of North-East Lancashire. Crown 8vo. Cloth, price 3*s. 6d.*

HAWEIS (Rev. H. R.), M.A.

Arrows in the Air. Crown 8vo. Second Edition. Cloth, price 6*s.*

Current Coin. Materialism— The Devil—Crime—Drunkenness— Pauperism—Emotion—Recreation— The Sabbath. Third Edition. Crown 8vo. Cloth, price 6*s.*

Speech in Season. Fourth Edition. Crown 8vo. Cloth, price 9*s.*

Thoughts for the Times. Eleventh Edition. Crown 8vo. Cloth, price 7*s. 6d.*

Unsectarian Family Prayers. New and Cheaper Edition. Fcap. 8vo. Cloth, price 1*s. 6d.*

HAWKER (Robert Stephen).

The Poetical Works of. Now first collected and arranged with a prefatory notice by J. G. Godwin. With Portrait. Crown 8vo. Cloth, price 12*s.*

HAWKINS (Edwards Comerford).

Spirit and Form. Sermons preached in the parish church of Leatherhead. Crown 8vo. Cloth, price 6*s.*

HAWTREY (Edward M.).

Corydalis. A Story of the Sicilian Expedition. Small crown 8vo. Cloth, price 3*s. 6d.*

HAYES (A. H.).

New Colorado and the Santa Fé Trail. With map and 60 Illustrations. Crown 8vo. Cloth, price 9*s.*

HEIDENHAIN (Rudolf), M.D.

Animal Magnetism. Physiological Observations. Translated from the Fourth German Edition, by L. C. Wooldridge. With a Preface by G. R. Romanes, F.R.S. Crown 8vo. Cloth, price 2*s. 6d.*

HELLWALD (Baron F. von).

The Russians in Central Asia. A Critical Examination, down to the present time, of the

HELLWALD (Baron F. von)— *continued.*

Geography and History of Central Asia. Translated by Lieut.-Col. Theodore Wirgman, LL.B. Large post 8vo. With Map. Cloth, price 12s.

HELVIG (Major H.).

The Operations of the Bavarian Army Corps. Translated by Captain G. S. Schwabe. With Five large Maps. In 2 vols. Demy 8vo. Cloth, price 24s.

Tactical Examples: Vol. I. The Battalion, price 15s. Vol. II. The Regiment and Brigade, price 10s. 6d. Translated from the German by Col. Sir Lumley Graham. With numerous Diagrams. Demy 8vo. Cloth.

HERFORD (Brooke).

The Story of Religion in England. A Book for Young Folk. Crown 8vo. Cloth, price 5s.

HINTON (James).

Life and Letters of. Edited by Ellice Hopkins, with an Introduction by Sir W. W. Gull, Bart., and Portrait engraved on Steel by C. H. Jeens. Second Edition. Crown 8vo. Cloth, 8s. 6d.

Chapters on the Art of Thinking, and other Essays. With an Introduction by Shadworth Hodgson. Edited by C. H. Hinton. Crown 8vo. Cloth, price 8s. 6d.

The Place of the Physician. To which is added Essays on the Law of Human Life, and on the Relation between Organic and Inorganic Worlds. Second Edition. Crown 8vo. Cloth, price 3s. 6d.

Physiology for Practical Use. By various Writers. With 50 Illustrations. Third and cheaper edition. Crown 8vo. Cloth, price 5s.

An Atlas of Diseases of the Membrana Tympani. With Descriptive Text. Post 8vo. Price £6 6s.

The Questions of Aural Surgery. With Illustrations. 2 vols. Post 8vo. Cloth, price 12s. 6d.

The Mystery of Pain. New Edition. Fcap. 8vo. Cloth limp, 1s.

HOCKLEY (W. B.).

Tales of the Zenana; or, A Nuwab's Leisure Hours. By the Author of "Pandurang Hari." With a Preface by Lord Stanley of Alderley. 2 vols. Crown 8vo. Cloth, price 21s.

Pandurang Hari; or, Memoirs of a Hindoo. A Tale of Mahratta Life sixty years ago. With a Preface by Sir H. Bartle E. Frere, G. C. S. I., &c. New and Cheaper Edition. Crown 8vo. Cloth, price 6s.

HOFFBAUER (Capt.).

The German Artillery in the Battles near Metz. Based on the official reports of the German Artillery. Translated by Capt. E. O. Hollist. With Map and Plans. Demy 8vo. Cloth, price 21s.

HOLMES (E. G. A.).

Poems. First and Second Series. Fcap. 8vo. Cloth, price 5s. each.

HOOPER (Mary).

Little Dinners: How to Serve them with Elegance and Economy. Thirteenth Edition. Crown 8vo. Cloth, price 5s.

Cookery for Invalids, Persons of Delicate Digestion, and Children. Crown 8vo. Cloth, price 3s. 6d.

Every-Day Meals. Being Economical and Wholesome Recipes for Breakfast, Luncheon, and Supper. Second Edition. Crown 8vo. Cloth, price 5s.

HOOPER (Mrs. G.).

The House of Raby. With a Frontispiece. Crown 8vo. Cloth, price 3s. 6d.

HOPKINS (Ellice).

Life and Letters of James Hinton, with an Introduction by Sir W. W. Gull, Bart., and Portrait engraved on Steel by C. H. Jeens. Second Edition. Crown 8vo. Cloth, price 8s. 6d.

HOPKINS (M.).

The Port of Refuge; or, Counsel and Aid to Shipmasters in Difficulty, Doubt, or Distress. Crown 8vo. Second and Revised Edition. Cloth, price 6s.

HORNER (The Misses).

Walks in Florence. A New
and thoroughly Revised Edition. 2 vols. Crown 8vo. Cloth limp. With Illustrations.
Vol. I.—Churches, Streets, and Palaces. 10s. 6d. Vol. II.—Public Galleries and Museums. 5s.

Household Readings on
Prophecy. By a Layman. Small crown 8vo. Cloth, price 3s. 6d.

HULL (Edmund C. P.).

The European in India.
With a MEDICAL GUIDE FOR ANGLO-INDIANS. By R. R. S. Mair, M.D., F.R.C.S.E. Third Edition, Revised and Corrected. Post 8vo. Cloth, price 6s.

HUTCHISON (Lieut.-Col. F. J.), and Capt.G. H. MACGREGOR.

Military Sketching and Re-
connaissance. With Fifteen Plates. Second edition. Small 8vo. Cloth, price 6s.
The first Volume of Military Handbooks for Regimental Officers. Edited by Lieut.-Col. C. B. BRACKENBURY, R.A., A.A.G.

HUTTON (Arthur), M.A.

The Anglican Ministry. Its
Nature and Value in relation to the Catholic Priesthood. With a Preface by his Eminence Cardinal Newman. Demy 8vo. Cloth, price 14s.

INCHBOLD (J. W.).

Annus Amoris. Sonnets.
Fcap. 8vo. Cloth, price 4s. 6d.

INGELOW (Jean).

Off the Skelligs. A Novel.
With Frontispiece. Second Edition. Crown 8vo. Cloth, price 6s.

The Little Wonder-horn.
A Second Series of "Stories Told to a Child." With Fifteen Illustrations. Small 8vo. Cloth, price 2s. 6d.

Indian Bishoprics. By an
Indian Churchman. Demy 8vo. 6d.

International Scientific
Series (The).
I. Forms of Water: A Familiar Exposition of the Origin and Phenomena of Glaciers. By J. Tyndall, LL.D., F.R.S. With 25 Illustrations. Seventh Edition. Crown 8vo. Cloth, price 5s.

International Scientific Series (The)—continued.
II. Physics and Politics; or, Thoughts on the Application of the Principles of "Natural Selection" and "Inheritance" to Political Society. By Walter Bagehot. Fifth Edition. Crown 8vo. Cloth, price 4s.

III. Foods. By Edward Smith, M.D., &c. With numerous Illustrations. Seventh Edition. Crown 8vo. Cloth, price 5s.

IV. Mind and Body: The Theories of their Relation. By Alexander Bain, LL.D. With Four Illustrations. Tenth Edition. Crown 8vo. Cloth, price 4s.

V. The Study of Sociology. By Herbert Spencer. Tenth Edition. Crown 8vo. Cloth, price 5s.

VI. On the Conservation of Energy. By Balfour Stewart, LL.D., &c. With 14 Illustrations. Fifth Edition. Crown 8vo. Cloth, price 5s.

VII. Animal Locomotion; or, Walking, Swimming, and Flying. By J. B. Pettigrew, M.D., &c. With 130 Illustrations. Second Edition. Crown 8vo. Cloth, price 5s.

VIII. Responsibility in Mental Disease. By Henry Maudsley, M.D. Third Edition. Crown 8vo. Cloth, price 5s.

IX. The New Chemistry. By Professor J. P. Cooke. With 31 Illustrations. Fifth Edition. Crown 8vo. Cloth, price 5s.

X. The Science of Law. By Prof. Sheldon Amos. Fourth Edition. Crown 8vo. Cloth, price 5s.

XI. Animal Mechanism. A Treatise on Terrestrial and Aerial Locomotion. By Prof. E. J. Marey. With 117 Illustrations. Second Edition. Crown 8vo. Cloth, price 5s.

XII. The Doctrine of Descent and Darwinism. By Prof. Osca Schmidt. With 26 Illustrations. Fourth Edition. Crown 8vo. Cloth, price 5s.

XIII. The History of the Conflict between Religion and Science. By J. W. Draper, M.D., LL.D. Fifteenth Edition. Crown 8vo. Cloth, price 5s.

International Scientific Series (The)—*continued*.

XIV. Fungi; their Nature, Influences, Uses, &c. By M. C. Cooke, LL.D. Edited by the Rev. M. J. Berkeley, F.L.S. With numerous Illustrations. Second Edition. Crown 8vo. Cloth, price 5s.

XV. The Chemical Effects of Light and Photography. By Dr. Hermann Vogel. With 100 Illustrations. Third and Revised Edition. Crown 8vo. Cloth, price 5s.

XVI. The Life and Growth of Language. By Prof. William Dwight Whitney. Third Edition. Crown 8vo. Cloth, price 5s.

XVII. Money and the Mechanism of Exchange. By W. Stanley Jevons, F.R.S. Fourth Edition. Crown 8vo. Cloth, price 5s.

XVIII. The Nature of Light: With a General Account of Physical Optics. By Dr. Eugene Lommel. With 188 Illustrations and a table of Spectra in Chromo-lithography. Third Edition. Crown 8vo. Cloth, price 5s.

XIX. Animal Parasites and Messmates. By M. Van Beneden. With 83 Illustrations. Second Edition. Crown 8vo. Cloth, price 5s.

XX. Fermentation. By Prof. Schützenberger. With 28 Illustrations. Third Edition. Crown 8vo. Cloth, price 5s.

XXI. The Five Senses of Man. By Prof. Bernstein. With 91 Illustrations. Second Edition. Crown 8vo. Cloth, price 5s.

XXII. The Theory of Sound in its Relation to Music. By Prof. Pietro Blaserna. With numerous Illustrations. Second Edition. Crown 8vo. Cloth, price 5s.

XXIII. Studies in Spectrum Analysis. By J. Norman Lockyer. F.R.S. With six photographic Illustrations of Spectra, and numerous engravings on wood. Crown 8vo. Second Edition. Cloth, price 6s. 6d.

XXIV. A History of the Growth of the Steam Engine. By Prof. R. H. Thurston. With numerous Illustrations. Second Edition. Crown 8vo. Cloth, price 6s. 6d.

XXV. Education as a Science. By Alexander Bain, LL.D. Third Edition. Crown 8vo. Cloth, price 5s.

International Scientific Series (The)—*continued*.

XXVI. The Human Species. By Prof. A. de Quatrefages. Third Edition. Crown 8vo. Cloth, price 5s.

XXVII. Modern Chromatics. With Applications to Art and Industry, by Ogden N. Rood. Second Edition. With 130 original Illustrations. Crown 8vo. Cloth, price 5s.

XXVIII. The Crayfish: an Introduction to the Study of Zoology. By Prof. T. H. Huxley. Third edition. With eighty-two Illustrations. Crown 8vo. Cloth, price 5s.

XXIX. The Brain as an Organ of Mind. By H. Charlton Bastian, M.D. With numerous Illustrations. Second Edition. Crown 8vo. Cloth, price 5s.

XXX. The Atomic Theory. By Prof. Ad. Wurtz. Translated by E. Clemin-Shaw. Second Edition. Crown 8vo. Cloth, price 5s.

XXXI. The Natural Conditions of Existence as they affect Animal Life. By Karl Semper. Second Edition. Crown 8vo. Cloth, price 5s.

XXXII. General Physiology of Muscles and Nerves. By Prof. J. Rosenthal. Second Edition, with illustrations. Crown 8vo. Cloth, price 5s.

XXXIII. Sight: an Exposition of the Principles of Monocular and Binocular Vision. By Joseph Le Conte, LL.D. With 132 illustrations. Crown 8vo. Cloth, price 5s.

XXXIV. Illusions: A Psychological Study. By James Sully. Crown 8vo. Cloth, price 5s.

XXXV. Volcanoes: What they are and What they Teach. By Prof. J. W. Judd, F.R.S. With 92 Illustrations on Wood. Crown 8vo. Cloth, price 5s.

JENKINS (E.) and RAYMOND (J.).
The Architect's Legal Handbook. Third Edition Revised. Crown 8vo. Cloth, price 6s.

JENKINS (Rev. R. C.), M.A.
The Privilege of Peter and the Claims of the Roman Church confronted with the Scriptures, the Councils, and the Testimony of the Popes themselves. Fcap. 8vo. Cloth, price 3s. 6d.

JENNINGS (Mrs. Vaughan).
Rahel : Her Life and Let-
ters. With a Portrait from the
Painting by Daffinger. Square post
8vo. Cloth, price 7s. 6d.

Jeroveam's Wife and other
Poems. Fcap. 8vo. Cloth, price
3s. 6d.

JOEL (L.).
A Consul's Manual and
Shipowner's and Shipmaster's Prac-
tical Guide in their Transactions
Abroad. With Definitions of Nauti-
cal, Mercantile, and Legal Terms;
a Glossary of Mercantile Terms in
English, French, German, Italian,
and Spanish. Tables of the Money,
Weights, and Measures of the Prin-
cipal Commercial Nations and their
Equivalents in British Standards ;
and Forms of Consular and Notarial
Acts. Demy 8vo. Cloth, price 12s.

JOHNSON (Virginia W.).
The Catskill Mountains.
Illustrated by Alfred Fredericks.
Cloth, price 5s.

JOHNSTONE (C. F.), M.A.
Historical Abstracts. Being
Outlines of the History of some of
the less-known States of Europe.
Crown 8vo. Cloth, price 7s. 6d.

JONES (Lucy).
Puddings and Sweets. Being
Three Hundred and Sixty-Five
Receipts approved by Experience.
Crown 8vo., price 2s. 6d.

JOYCE (P. W.), LL.D., &c.
Old Celtic Romances.
Translated from the Gaelic by.
Crown 8vo. Cloth, price 7s. 6d.

KAUFMANN (Rev. M.), B.A.
Utopias ; or, Schemes of
Social Improvement, from Sir
Thomas More to Karl Marx. Crown
8vo. Cloth, price 5s.

Socialism : Its Nature, its
Dangers, and its Remedies considered. Crown 8vo. Cloth, price 7s. 6d.

KAY (Joseph), M.A., Q.C.
Free Trade in Land.
Edited by his Widow. With Preface
by the Right Hon. John Bright,
M.P. Sixth Edition. Crown 8vo.
Cloth, price 5s.

KENT (Carolo).
Carona Catholica ad Petri
successoris Pedes Oblata. De
Summi Pontificis Leonis XIII. As-
sumptione Epiggramma. In Quin-
quaginta Linguis. Fcap. 4to. Cloth,
price 15s.

KER (David).
The Boy Slave in Bokhara.
A Tale of Central Asia. With Illustra-
tions. Crown 8vo. Cloth, price 3s. 6d.

The Wild Horseman of
the Pampas. Illustrated. Crown
8vo. Cloth, price 3s. 6d.

KERNER (Dr. A.), Professor of
Botany in the University of
Innsbruck.

Flowers and their Unbidden
Guests. Translation edited by W.
OGLE, M.A., M.D., and a prefatory
letter by C. Darwin, F.R.S. With Illustrations. Sq. 8vo. Cloth, price 9s.

KIDD (Joseph), M.D.
The Laws of Therapeutics,
or, the Science and Art of Medicine.
Second Edition. Crown 8vo. Cloth,
price 6s.

KINAHAN (G. Henry), M.R.I.A.,
&c., of her Majesty's Geological
Survey.
Manual of the Geology of
Ireland. With 8 Plates, 26 Woodcuts, and a Map of Ireland, geologi-
cally coloured. Square 8vo. Cloth,
price 15s.

KING (Mrs. Hamilton).
The Disciples. Fourth Edi-
tion, with Portrait and Notes.
Crown 8vo. Cloth, price 7s. 6d.

Aspromonte, and other
Poems. Second Edition. Fcap.
8vo. Cloth, price 4s. 6d.

KING (Edward).
Echoes from the Orient.
With Miscellaneous Poems. Small
crown 8vo. Cloth, price 3s. 6d.

KINGSLEY (Charles), M.A.
Letters and Memories of
his Life. Edited by his WIFE.
With 2 Steel engraved Portraits and
numerous Illustrations on Wood, and
a Facsimile of his Handwriting.

KINGSLEY (Charles), M.A.—
continued.

Thirteenth Edition. 2 vols. Demy 8vo. Cloth, price 36s.
** Also the ninth Cabinet Edition in 2 vols. Crown 8vo. Cloth, price 12s.

All Saints' Day and other Sermons. Second Edition. Crown 8vo. Cloth, 7s. 6d.

True Words for Brave Men: a Book for Soldiers' and Sailors' Libraries. Eighth Edition. Crown 8vo. Cloth, price 2s. 6d.

KNIGHT (Professor W.).
Studies in Philosophy and Literature. Large post 8vo. Cloth, price 7s. 6d.

KNOX (Alexander A.).
The New Playground : or, Wanderings in Algeria. Large crown 8vo. Cloth, price 10s. 6d.

LACORDAIRE (Rev. Père).
Life : Conferences delivered at Toulouse. A New and Cheaper Edition. Crown 8vo. Cloth, price 3s. 6d.

LAIRD-CLOWES (W.).
Love's Rebellion: a Poem. Fcap. 8vo. Cloth, price 3s. 6d.

LAMONT (Martha MacDonald).
The Gladiator : A Life under the Roman Empire in the beginning of the Third Century. With four Illustrations by H. M. Paget. Extra fcap. 8vo. Cloth, price 3s. 6d.

LANG (A.).
XXXII Ballades in Blue China. Elzevir. 8vo. Parchment, price 5s.

LAYMANN (Capt.).
The Frontal Attack of Infantry. Translated by Colonel Edward Newdigate. Crown 8vo. Cloth, price 2s. 6d.

LEANDER (Richard).
Fantastic Stories. Translated from the German by Paulina B. Granville. With Eight full-page Illustrations by M. E. Fraser-Tytler. Crown 8vo. Cloth, price 5s.

LEE (Rev. F. G.), D.C.L.
The Other World ; or, Glimpses of the Supernatural. 2 vols. A New Edition. Crown 8vo. Cloth, price 15s.

LEE (Holme).
Her Title of Honour. A Book for Girls. New Edition. With a Frontispiece. Crown 8vo. Cloth, price 5s.

LEIGH (Arran and Isla).
Bellerophôn. Small crown 8vo. Cloth, price 5s.

LEIGHTON (Robert).
Records and other Poems. With Portrait. Small crown 8vo. Cloth, price 7s. 6d.

LEWIS (Edward Dillon).
A Draft Code of Criminal Law and Procedure. Demy 8vo. Cloth, price 21s.

LEWIS (Mary A.).
A Rat with Three Tales. New and cheaper edition. With Four Illustrations by Catherine F. Frere. Crown 8vo. Cloth, price 3s. 6d.

LINDSAY (W. Lauder), M.D., &c.
Mind in the Lower Animals in Health and Disease. 2 vols. Demy 8vo. Cloth, price 32s.

LLOYD (Francis) and Charles Tebbitt.
Extension of Empire Weakness? Deficits Ruin? With a Practical Scheme for the Reconstruction of Asiatic Turkey. Small crown 8vo. Cloth, price 3s. 6d.

LOCKER (F.).
London Lyrics. A New and Revised Edition, with Additions and a Portrait of the Author. Crown 8vo. Cloth, elegant, price 6s.

LOKI.
The New Werther. Small crown 8vo. Cloth, price 2s. 6d.

LORIMER (Peter), D.D.
John Knox and the Church of England : His Work in her Pulpit, and his Influence upon her Liturgy, Articles, and Parties. Demy 8vo. Cloth, price 12s.

John Wiclif and his English Precursors, by Gerhard Victor Lechler. Translated from the German, with additional Notes. 2 vols. Demy 8vo. Cloth, price 21s.

Love's Gamut and other Poems. Small crown 8vo. Cloth, price 3s. 6d.

Love Sonnets of Proteus.
With frontispiece by the Author.
Elzevir 8vo. Cloth, price 5s.

LOWNDES (Henry).
Poems and Translations.
Crown 8vo. Cloth, price 6s.

LUMSDEN (Lieut.-Col. H. W.).
Beowulf. An Old English
Poem. Translated into modern
rhymes. Small crown 8vo. Cloth,
price 5s.

MAC CLINTOCK (L.).
**Sir Spangle and the Dingy
Hen.** Illustrated. Square crown
8vo., price 2s. 6d.

MACDONALD (G.).
Malcolm. With Portrait of
the Author engraved on Steel. Fourth
Edition. Crown 8vo. Price 6s.
The Marquis of Lossie.
Second Edition. Crown 8vo. Cloth,
price 6s.
St. George and St. Michael.
Second Edition. Crown 8vo. Cloth, 6s.

MACKENNA (S. J.).
Plucky Fellows. A Book
for Boys. With Six Illustrations.
Fourth Edition. Crown 8vo. Cloth,
price 3s. 6d.
**At School with an Old
Dragoon.** With Six Illustrations.
Second Edition. Crown 8vo. Cloth,
price 5s.

MACLACHLAN (Mrs.).
Notes and Extracts on
Everlasting Punishment and
Eternal Life, according to
Literal Interpretation. Small
crown 8vo. Cloth, price 3s. 6d.

MACLEAN (Charles Donald).
Latin and Greek Verse
Translations. Small crown 8vo.
Cloth, price 2s.

MACNAUGHT (Rev. John).
Cœna Domini: An Essay
on the Lord's Supper, its Primitive Institution, Apostolic Uses,
and Subsequent History. Demy
8vo. Cloth, price 14s.

MAGNUS (Mrs.).
About the Jews since Bible
Times. From the Babylonian exile
till the English Exodus. Small
crown 8vo. Cloth, price 5s.

**MAGNUSSON (Eirikr), M.A.,
and PALMER (E.H.), M.A.**
Johan Ludvig Runeberg's
Lyrical Songs, Idylls and Epigrams. Fcap. 8vo. Cloth, price 5s.

MAIR (R. S.), M.D., F.R.C.S.E.
The Medical Guide for
Anglo-Indians. Being a Compendium of Advice to Europeans in
India, relating to the Preservation
and Regulation of Health. With a
Supplement on the Management of
Children in India. Second Edition.
Crown 8vo. Limp cloth, price 3s. 6d.

MALDEN (H. E. and E. E.)
Princes and Princesses.
Illustrated. Small crown 8vo. Cloth,
price 2s. 6d.

MANNING (His Eminence Cardinal).
The True Story of the
Vatican Council. Crown 8vo.
Cloth, price 5s.
Marie Antoinette: a Drama.
Small crown 8vo. Cloth, price 5s.

MARKHAM (Capt. Albert Hastings), R.N.
The Great Frozen Sea. A
Personal Narrative of the Voyage of
the "Alert" during the Arctic Expedition of 1875-6. With six fullpage Illustrations, two Maps, and
twenty-seven Woodcuts. Fourth
and cheaper edition. Crown 8vo.
Cloth, price 6s.
A Polar Reconnaissance:
being the Voyage of the "Isbjorn"
to Novaya Zemlya in 1879. With
10 Illustrations. Demy 8vo. Cloth,
price 16s.

MARTINEAU (Gertrude).
Outline Lessons on
Morals. Small crown 8vo. Cloth,
price 3s. 6d.

Master Bobby: a Tale. By
the Author of "Christina North."
With Illustrations by E. H. BELL.
Extra fcap. 8vo. Cloth, price 3s.6d.

MASTERMAN (J.).
Half-a-dozen Daughters.
With a Frontispiece. Crown 8vo.
Cloth, price 3s. 6d.

McGRATH (Terence).

Pictures from Ireland. New and cheaper edition. Crown 8vo. Cloth, price 2s.

MEREDITH (George).

The Egoist. A Comedy in Narrative. 3 vols. Crown 8vo. Cloth.

** Also a Cheaper Edition, with Frontispiece. Crown 8vo. Cloth, price 6s.

The Ordeal of Richard Feverel. A History of Father and Son. In one vol. with Frontispiece. Crown 8vo. Cloth, price 6s.

MERRITT (Henry).

Art - Criticism and Romance. With Recollections, and Twenty-three Illustrations in *eau-forte*, by Anna Lea Merritt. Two vols. Large post 8vo. Cloth, 25s.

MIDDLETON (The Lady).

Ballads. Square 16mo. Cloth, price 3s. 6d.

MILLER (Edward).

The History and Doctrines of Irvingism; or, the so-called Catholic and Apostolic Church. 2 vols. Large post 8vo. Cloth, price 25s.

The Church in Relation to the State. Crown 8vo. Cloth, price 7s. 6d.

MILNE (James).

Tables of Exchange for the Conversion of Sterling Money into Indian and Ceylon Currency, at Rates from 1s. 8d. to 2s. 3d. per Rupee. Second Edition. Demy 8vo. Cloth, price £2 2s.

MINCHIN (J. G.).

Bulgaria since the War. Notes of a Tour in the Autumn of 1879. Small crown 8vo. Cloth, price 3s. 6d.

MOCKLER (E.).

A Grammar of the Baloo- chee Language, as it is spoken in Makran (Ancient Gedrosia), in the Persia-Arabic and Roman characters. Fcap. 8vo. Cloth, price 5s.

MOFFAT (Robert Scott).

The Economy of Consump- tion; an Omitted Chapter in Political Economy, with special reference to the Questions of Commercial Crises and the Policy of Trades Unions; and with Reviews of the Theories of Adam Smith, Ricardo, J. S. Mill, Fawcett, &c. Demy 8vo. Cloth, price 18s.

The Principles of a Time Policy: being an Exposition of a Method of Settling Disputes between Employers and Employed in regard to Time and Wages, by a simple Process of Mercantile Barter, without recourse to Strikes or Locks-out. Demy 8vo. Cloth, price 3s. 6d.

Monmouth: A Drama, of which the Outline is Historical. Dedicated by permission to Mr. Henry Irving. Small crown 8vo. Cloth, price 5s.

MOORE (Mrs. Bloomfield).

Gondaline's Lesson. The Warden's Tale, Stories for Children, and other Poems. Crown 8vo. Cloth, price 5s.

MORELL (J. R.).

Euclid Simplified in Me- thod and Language. Being a Manual of Geometry. Compiled from the most important French Works, approved by the University of Paris and the Minister of Public Instruction. Fcap. 8vo. Cloth, price 2s. 6d.

MORICE (Rev. F. D.), M.A.

The Olympian and Pythian Odes of Pindar. A New Translation in English Verse. Crown 8vo. Cloth, price 7s. 6d.

MORSE (E. S.), Ph.D.

First Book of Zoology. With numerous Illustrations. New and cheaper edition. Crown 8vo. Cloth, price 2s. 6d.

MORSHEAD (E. D. A.)

The House of Atreus. Being the Agamemnon Libation-Bearers and Furies of Æschylus Translated into English Verse. Crown 8vo. Cloth, price 7s.

MORTERRA (Felix).

The Legend of Allandale, and other Poems. Small crown 8vo. Cloth, price 6s.

MUNRO (Major-Gen. Sir Thomas), K.C.B., Governor of Madras.

Selections from His Minutes, and other Official Writings. Edited, with an Introductory Memoir, by Sir Alexander Arbuthnot, K.C.S.I., C.I.E. Two vols. Demy 8vo. Cloth, price 30s.

NAAKE (J. T.).

Slavonic Fairy Tales. From Russian, Servian, Polish, and Bohemian Sources. With Four Illustrations. Crown 8vo. Cloth, price 5s.

NADEN (Constance W.).

Songs and Sonnets of Spring-Time. Small crown 8vo. Cloth, price 5s.

NEWMAN (J. H.), D.D.

Characteristics from the Writings of. Being Selections from his various Works. Arranged with the Author's personal approval. Third Edition. With Portrait. Crown 8vo. Cloth, price 6s.

₊ A Portrait of the Rev. Dr. J. H. Newman, mounted for framing, can be had. price 2s. 6d.

NICHOLAS (Thomas), Ph.D., F.G.S.

The Pedigree of the English People: an Argument, Historical and Scientific, on the Formation and Growth of the Nation, tracing Race-admixture in Britain from the earliest times, with especial reference to the incorporation of the Celtic Aborigines. Fifth Edition. Demy 8vo. Cloth, price 16s.

NICHOLSON (Edward Byron).

The Christ Child, and other Poems. Crown 8vo. Cloth, price 4s. 6d.

The Rights of an Animal. Crown 8vo. Cloth, price 3s. 6d.

The Gospel according to the Hebrews. Its Fragments translated and annotated, with a critical Analysis of the External and Internal Evidence relating to it. Demy 8vo. Cloth, price 9s. 6d.

A New Commentary on the Gospel according to Matthew. Demy 8vo. Cloth, price 12s.

NICOLS (Arthur), F.G.S., F.R.G.S.

Chapters from the Physical History of the Earth. An Introduction to Geology and Palæontology, with numerous illustrations. Crown 8vo. Cloth, price 5s.

NOAKE (Major R. Compton).

The Bivouac ; or, Martial Lyrist, with an Appendix—Advice to the Soldier. Fcap. 8vo. Price 5s. 6d.

NOEL (The Hon. Roden).

A Little Child's Monument. Small crown 8vo. Cloth, price 3s. 6d.

NORMAN PEOPLE (The).

The Norman People, and their Existing Descendants in the British Dominions and the United States of America. Demy 8vo. Cloth, price 21s.

NORRIS (Rev. Alfred).

The Inner and Outer Life Poems. Fcap. 8vo. Cloth, price 6s.

Notes on Cavalry Tactics, Organization, &c. By a Cavalry Officer. With Diagrams. Demy 8vo. Cloth, price 12s.

Nuces : Exercises on the Syntax of the Public School Latin Primer. New Edition in Three Parts. Crown 8vo. Each 1s.

₊ The Three Parts can also be had bound together in cloth, price 3s.

OATES (Frank), F.R.G.S.

Matabele Land and the Victoria Falls: A Naturalist's Wanderings in the Interior of South Africa. Edited by C. G. Oates, B.A., with numerous illustrations and four maps. Demy 8vo. Cloth.

O'BRIEN (Charlotte G.).

Light and Shade. 2 vols. Crown 8vo. Cloth, gilt tops, price 12s.

Ode of Life (The). Third Edition. Fcap. 8vo. Cloth, price 5s.

OF THE IMITATION OF CHRIST. Four books. Demy 32mo. Limp cloth, price 1s.

₊ Also in various bindings.

O'HAGAN (John).

The Song of Roland. Translated into English Verse. Large post 8vo. Parchment antique, price 10s. 6d.

O'MEARA (Kathleen).

Frederic Ozanam, Professor of the Sorbonne ; His Life and Works. Second Edition. Crown 8vo. Cloth, price 7s. 6d.

Henri Perreyve and His Counsels to the Sick. Small crown 8vo. Cloth, price 5s.

Our Public Schools. Eton, Harrow, Winchester, Rugby, Westminster, Marlborough, The Charterhouse. Crown 8vo. Cloth, price 6s.

OWEN (F. M.).

John Keats. A Study. Crown 8vo. Cloth, price 6s.

OWEN (Rev. Robert), B.D.

Sanctorale Catholicum ; or Book of Saints. With Notes, Critical, Exegetical, and Historical. Demy 8vo. Cloth, price 18s.

An Essay on the Communion of Saints. Including an Examination of the "Cultus Sanctorum." Price 2s.

PALGRAVE (W. Gifford).

Hermann Agha ; An Eastern Narrative. Third and Cheaper Edition. Crown 8vo. Cloth, price 6s.

PANDURANG HARI ;

Or, Memoirs of a Hindoo. With an Introductory Preface by Sir H. Bartle E. Frere, G.C.S.I., C B. Crown 8vo. Price 6s.

PARCHMENT LIBRARY (The).

Choicely printed on hand-made paper, limp parchment antique, price 6s. each ; vellum, price 7s. 6d. each.

Shakspere's Sonnets. Edited by Edward Dowden, Author of "Shakspere ; his Mind and Art," &c. With a Frontispiece, etched by Leopold Lowenstam, after the Death Mask.

English Odes. Selected by Edmund W. Gosse, Author of "Studies in the Literature of Northern Europe." With Frontispiece on India paper by Hamo Thornycroft, A.R.A.

PARCHMENT LIBRARY (The)
— *continued*.

Of the Imitation of Christ. By Thomas à Kempis. A revised Translation. With Frontispiece on India paper, from a Design by W. B. Richmond.

Tennyson's The Princess : a Medley. With a Miniature Frontispiece by H. M. Paget, and a Tailpiece in Outline by Gordon Browne.

Poems : Selected from Percy Bysshe Shelley. Dedicated to Lady Shelley. With Preface by Richard Garnet, and a Miniature Frontispiece.

Tennyson's "In Memoriam." With a Miniature Portrait in *eau forte* by Le Rat, after a Photograph by the late Mrs. Cameron.

PARKER (Joseph), D.D.

The Paraclete : An Essay on the Personality and Ministry of the Holy Ghost, with some reference to current discussions. Second Edition. Demy 8vo. Cloth, price 12s.

PARR (Capt. H. Hallam).

A Sketch of the Kafir and Zulu Wars : Guadana to Isandhlwana, with Maps. Small crown 8vo. Cloth, price 5s.

The Dress, Horses, and Equipment of Infantry and Staff Officers. Crown 8vo. Cloth, price 1s.

PARSLOE (Joseph).

Our Railways : Sketches, Historical and Descriptive. With Practical Information as to Fares, Rates, &c., and a Chapter on Railway Reform. Crown 8vo. Cloth, price 6s.

PATTISON (Mrs. Mark).

The Renaissance of Art in France. With Nineteen Steel Engravings. 2 vols. Demy 8vo. Cloth, price 32s.

PAUL (C. Kegan).

Mary Wollstonecraft. Letters to Imlay. With Prefatory Memoir by, and Two Portraits in *eau forte*, by Anna Lea Merritt. Crown 8vo. Cloth, price 6s.

PAUL (C. Kegan)—*continued.*
Goethe's Faust. A New
Translation in Rime. Crown 8vo. Cloth, price 6s.
William Godwin: His
Friends and Contemporaries. With Portraits and Facsimiles of the Handwriting of Godwin and his Wife. 2 vols. Square post 8vo. Cloth, price 28s.
The Genius of Christianity
Unveiled. Being Essays by William Godwin never before published. Edited, with a Preface, by C. Kegan Paul. Crown 8vo. Cloth, price 7s. 6d.

PAUL (Margaret Agnes).
Gentle and Simple: A Story.
2 vols. Crown 8vo. Cloth, gilt tops, price 12s.
*** Also a Cheaper Edition in one vol. with Frontispiece. Crown 8vo. Cloth, price 6s.

PAYNE (John).
Songs of Life and Death.
Crown 8vo. Cloth, price 5s.

PAYNE (Prof. J. F.).
Fröbel and the Kindergarten System. Second Edition.
A Visit to German Schools:
Elementary Schools in Germany. Notes of a Professional Tour to inspect some of the Kindergartens, Primary Schools, Public Girls' Schools, and Schools for Technical Instruction in Hamburgh, Berlin, Dresden, Weimar, Gotha, Eisenach, in the autumn of 1874. With Critical Discussions of the General Principles and Practice of Kindergartens and other Schemes of Elementary Education. Crown 8vo. Cloth, price 4s. 6d.

PELLETAN (E.).
The Desert Pastor, Jean
Jarousseau. Translated from the French. By Colonel E. P. De L'Hoste. With a Frontispiece. New Edition. Fcap. 8vo. Cloth, price 3s. 6d.

PENNELL (H. Cholmondeley).
Pegasus Resaddled. By
the Author of " Puck on Pegasus," &c. &c. With Ten Full-page Illustrations by George Du Maurier. Second Edition. Fcap. 4to. Cloth elegant, price 12s. 6d.

PENRICE (Maj. J.), B.A.
A Dictionary and Glossary
of the Ko-ran. With copious Grammatical References and Explanations of the Text. 4to. Cloth, price 21s.

PESCHEL (Dr. Oscar).
The Races of Man and
their Geographical Distribution. Large crown 8vo. Cloth, price 9s.

PETERS (F. H.).
The Nicomachean Ethics
of Aristotle. Translated by. Crown 8vo. Cloth, price 6s.

PFEIFFER (Emily).
Quarterman's Grace, and
other Poems. Crown 8vo. Cloth, price 5s.
Glan Alarch: His Silence
and Song. A Poem. Second Edition. Crown 8vo. price 6s.
Gerard's Monument, and
other Poems. Second Edition. Crown 8vo. Cloth, price 6s.
Poems. Second Edition.
Crown 8vo. Cloth, price 6s.
Sonnets and Songs. New
Edition. 16mo, handsomely printed and bound in cloth, gilt edges, price 5s.

PIKE (Warburton).
The Inferno of Dante Ali-
ghieri. Demy 8vo. Cloth, price 5s.

PINCHES (Thomas), M.A.
Samuel Wilberforce: Faith
—Service—Recompense. Three Sermons. With a Portrait of Bishop Wilberforce (after a Photograph by Charles Watkins). Crown 8vo. Cloth, price 4s. 6d.

PLAYFAIR (Lieut.-Col.), Her Britannic Majesty's Consul-General in Algiers.
Travels in the Footsteps of
Bruce in Algeria and Tunis. Illustrated by facsimiles of Bruce's original Drawings, Photographs, Maps, &c. Royal 4to. Cloth, bevelled boards, gilt leaves, price £3 3s.

POLLOCK (Frederick).
Spinoza. His Life and Phi-
losophy. Demy 8vo. Cloth, price 16s.

POLLOCK (W. H.).
Lectures on French Poets.
Delivered at the Royal Institution.
Small crown 8vo. Cloth, price 5s.

POOR (Laura E.).
Sanskrit and its kindred
Literatures. Studies in Compara-
tive Mythology. Small crown 8vo.
Cloth, price 5s.

POUSHKIN (A. S.).
Russian Romance.
Translated from the Tales of Belkin,
&c. By Mrs. J. Buchan Telfer (née
Mouravieff). Crown 8vo. Cloth,
price 3s. 6d.

PRESBYTER.
Unfoldings of Christian
Hope. An Essay showing that the
Doctrine contained in the Damna-
tory Clauses of the Creed commonly
called Athanasian is unscriptural.
Small crown 8vo. Cloth, price 4s. 6d.

PRICE (Prof. Bonamy).
Currency and Banking.
Crown 8vo. Cloth, price 6s.

Chapters on Practical Political Economy. Being the Substance of Lectures delivered before
the University of Oxford. Large
post 8vo. Cloth, price 12s.

Proteus and Amadeus. A
Correspondence. Edited by Aubrey
De Vere. Crown 8vo. Cloth, price 5s.

PUBLIC SCHOOLBOY.
The Volunteer, the Militia-
man, and the Regular Soldier.
Crown 8vo. Cloth, price 5s.

PULPIT COMMENTARY (The).
Edited by the Rev. J. S. EXELL and
the Rev. Canon H. D. M. SPENCE.
Genesis. By Rev. T. White-
law, M.A.; with Homilies by the
Very Rev. J. F. Montgomery, D.D.,
Rev. Prof. R. A. Redford, M.A.,
LL.B., Rev. F. Hastings, Rev. W.
Roberts, M.A. An Introduction to
the Study of the Old Testament by
the Rev. Canon Farrar, D.D.,
F.R.S.; and Introductions to the
Pentateuch by the Right Rev. H.
Cotterill, D.D., and Rev. T. White-
law, M.A. Fourth Edition. Price
15s.

PULPIT COMMENTARY (The)
—*continued.*
Numbers. By the Rev. R.
Winterbotham, LL.B. With Homilies
by the Rev. Prof. W. Binnie, D.D.,
Rev. E. S. Prout, M.A., Rev. D.
Young, Rev. J. Waite, and an In-
troduction by the Rev. Thomas
Whitelaw, M.A. Price 15s.

Joshua. By the Rev. J. J.
Lias, M.A. With Homilies by the
Rev. S. R. Aldridge, LL.B., Rev.
R. Glover, Rev. E. de Pressensé,
D.D., Rev. J. Waite, Rev. F. W.
Adeney, and an Introduction by the
Rev. A. Plummer, M.A. Second
Edition. Price 12s. 6d.

Judges and Ruth. By Right
Rev. Lord A. C. Hervey, D.D., and
Rev. J. Morrison, D.D. With Ho-
milies by Rev. A. F. Muir, M.A.;
Rev. W. F. Adeney, M.A.; Rev.
W. M. Statham; and Rev. Prof. J.
R. Thomson, M.A. Second Edition.
Cloth, price 15s.

1 Samuel. By the Very Rev.
R. P. Smith, D.D. With Homilies
by the Rev. Donald Fraser, D.D.,
Rev. Prof. Chapman, and Rev. B.
Dale. Third Edition. Price 15s.

Ezra, Nehemiah, and
Esther. By Rev. Canon G. Rawlin-
son, M.A.; with Homilies by Rev.
Prof. J. R. Thomson, M.A., Rev.
Prof. R. A. Redford, LL.B., M.A.,
Rev. W. S. Lewis, M.A., Rev. J. A.
Macdonald, Rev. A. Mackennal,
B.A., Rev. W. Clarkson, B.A., Rev.
F. Hastings, Rev. W. Dinwiddie,
LL.B., Rev. Prof. Rowlands, B.A.,
Rev. G. Wood, B.A., Rev. Prof. P.
C. Barker, LL.B., M.A., and Rev.
J. S. Exell. Fourth Edition. Price
12s. 6d.

Punjaub (The) and North
Western Frontier of India. By an
old Punjaubee. Crown 8vo. Cloth,
price 5s.

Rabbi Jeshua. An Eastern
Story. Crown 8vo. Cloth, price
3s. 6d.

**RAVENSHAW (John Henry),
B.C.S.**
Gaur: Its Ruins and In-
scriptions. Edited with consider-

RAVENSHAW (John Henry), B.C.S.—*continued.*

able additions and alterations by his Widow. With forty-four photographic illustrations and twenty-five fac-similes of Inscriptions. Super royal 4to. Cloth, 3*l.* 13*s.* 6*d.*

READ (Carveth).

On the Theory of Logic : An Essay. Crown 8vo. Cloth, price 6*s.*

Realities of the Future Life. Small crown 8vo. Cloth, price 1*s.* 6*d.*

REANEY (Mrs. G. S.).

Blessing and Blessed ; a Sketch of Girl Life. New and cheaper Edition. With a frontispiece. Crown 8vo. Cloth, price 3*s.* 6*d.*

Waking and Working ; or, from Girlhood to Womanhood. New and cheaper edition. With a Frontispiece. Crown 8vo. Cloth, price 3*s.* 6*d.*

Rose Gurney's Discovery. A Book for Girls, dedicated to their Mothers. Crown 8vo. Cloth, price 3*s.* 6*d.*

English Girls : their Place and Power. With a Preface by R. W. Dale, M.A., of Birmingham. Third Edition. Fcap. 8vo. Cloth, price 2*s.* 6*d.*

Just Anyone, and other Stories. Three Illustrations. Royal 16mo. Cloth, price 1*s.* 6*d.*

Sunshine Jenny and other Stories. Three Illustrations. Royal 16mo. Cloth, price 1*s.* 6*d.*

Sunbeam Willie, and other Stories. Three Illustrations. Royal 16mo. Cloth, price 1*s.* 6*d.*

RENDALL (J. M.).

Concise Handbook of the Island of Madeira. With plan of Funchal and map of the Island. Fcap. 8vo. Cloth, price 1*s.* 6*d.*

REYNOLDS (Rev. J. W.).

The Supernatural in Na- ture. A Verification by Free Use of Science. Second Edition, revised and enlarged. Demy 8vo. Cloth, price 14*s.*

Mystery of Miracles, The. By the Author of "The Supernatural in Nature." Crown 8vo. Cloth, price 6*s.*

RHOADES (James).

The Georgics of Virgil. Translated into English Verse. Small crown 8vo. Cloth, price 5*s.*

RIBOT (Prof. Th.).

English Psychology. Second Edition. A Revised and Corrected Translation from the latest French Edition. Large post 8vo. Cloth, price 9*s.*

Heredity : A Psychological Study on its Phenomena, its Laws, its Causes, and its Consequences. Large crown 8vo. Cloth, price 9*s.*

RINK (Chevalier Dr. Henry).

Greenland : Its People and its Products. By the Chevalier Dr. HENRY RINK, President of the Greenland Board of Trade. With sixteen Illustrations, drawn by the Eskimo, and a Map. Edited by Dr. ROBERT BROWN. Crown 8vo. Price 10*s.* 6*d.*

ROBERTSON (The Late Rev. F. W.), M.A., of Brighton.

The Human Race, and other Sermons preached at Cheltenham, Oxford, and Brighton. Second Edition. Large post 8vo. Cloth, price 7*s.* 6*d.*

Notes on Genesis. New and cheaper Edition. Crown 8vo., price 3*s.* 6*d.*

Sermons. Four Series. Small crown 8vo. Cloth, price 3*s.* 6*d.* each.

Expository Lectures on St. Paul's Epistles to the Corinthians. A New Edition. Small crown 8vo. Cloth, price 5*s.*

Lectures and Addresses, with other literary remains. A New Edition. Crown 8vo. Cloth, price 5*s.*

An Analysis of Mr. Tenny- son's "In Memoriam." (Dedicated by Permission to the Poet-Laureate.) Fcap. 8vo. Cloth, price 2*s.*

The Education of the Human Race. Translated from the German of Gotthold Ephraim Lessing. Fcap. 8vo. Cloth, price 2*s.* 6*d.*

Life and Letters. Edited by the Rev. Stopford Brooke, M.A., Chaplain in Ordinary to the Queen. I. 2 vols., uniform with the Sermons. With Steel Portrait. Crown 8vo. Cloth, price 7*s.* 6*d.*

ROBERTSON (The Late Rev. F. W.), M.A., of Brighton—*continued.*
II. Library Edition, in Demy 8vo., with Portrait. Cloth, price 12s.
III. A Popular Edition, in one vol. Crown 8vo. Cloth, price 6s.

The above Works can also be had half-bound in morocco.

*** A Portrait of the late Rev. F. W. Robertson, mounted for framing, can be had, price 2s. 6d.

ROBINSON (A. Mary F.).
A Handful of Honey-suckle. Fcap. 8vo. Cloth, price 3s. 6d.

The Crowned Hippolytus. Translated from Euripides. With New Poems. Small crown 8vo. Cloth, price 5s.

RODWELL (G. F.), F.R.A.S., F.C.S.
Etna: a History of the Mountain and its Eruptions. With Maps and Illustrations. Square 8vo. Cloth, price 9s.

ROSS (Mrs. E.), ("Nelsie Brook").
Daddy's Pet. A Sketch from Humble Life. With Six Illustrations. Royal 16mo. Cloth, price 1s.

ROSS (Alexander), D.D.
Memoir of Alexander Ewing, Bishop of Argyll and the Isles. Second and Cheaper Edition. Demy 8vo. Cloth, price 10s. 6d.

SADLER (S. W.), R.N.
The African Cruiser. A Midshipman's Adventures on the West Coast. With Three Illustrations. Second Edition. Crown 8vo. Cloth, price 3s. 6d.

SALTS (Rev. Alfred), LL.D.
Godparents at Confirmation. With a Preface by the Bishop of Manchester. Small crown 8vo. Cloth, limp, price 2s.

SALVATOR (Archduke Ludwig).
Levkosia, the Capital of Cyprus. Crown 8vo. Cloth, price 10s. 6d.

SAMUEL (Sydney Montagu).
Jewish Life in the East. Small crown 8vo. Cloth, price 3s. 6d.

SAUNDERS (John).
Israel Mort, Overman: A Story of the Mine. Cr. 8vo. Price 6s.

SAUNDERS (John)—*continued.*
Hirell. With Frontispiece. Crown 8vo. Cloth, price 3s. 6d.
Abel Drake's Wife. With Frontispiece. Crown 8vo. Cloth, price 3s. 6d.

SAYCE (Rev. Archibald Henry).
Introduction to the Science of Language. Two vols., large post 8vo. Cloth, price 25s.

SCHELL (Maj. von).
The Operations of the First Army under Gen. von Goeben. Translated by Col. C. H. von Wright. Four Maps. Demy 8vo. Cloth, price 9s.

The Operations of the First Army under Gen. von Steinmetz. Translated by Captain E. O. Hollist. Demy 8vo. Cloth, price 10s. 6d.

SCHELLENDORF (Maj.-Gen. B. von).
The Duties of the General Staff. Translated from the German by Lieutenant Hare. Vol. I. Demy 8vo. Cloth, 10s. 6d.

SCHERFF (Maj. W. von).
Studies in the New Infantry Tactics. Parts I. and II. Translated from the German by Colonel Lumley Graham. Demy 8vo. Cloth, price 7s. 6d.

Scientific Layman. The New Truth and the Old Faith: are they Incompatible? Demy 8vo. Cloth, price 10s. 6d.

SCOONES (W. Baptiste).
Four Centuries of English Letters. A Selection of 350 Letters by 150 Writers from the period of the Paston Letters to the Present Time. Edited and arranged by. Second Edition. Large crown 8vo. Cloth, price 9s.

SCOTT (Leader).
A Nook in the Apennines: A Summer beneath the Chestnuts. With Frontispiece, and 27 Illustrations in the Text, chiefly from Original Sketches. Crown 8vo. Cloth, price 7s. 6d.

SCOTT (Robert H.).
Weather Charts and Storm Warnings. Illustrated. Second Edition. Crown 8vo. Cloth, price 3s. 6d.

Seeking his Fortune, and other Stories. With Four Illustrations. New and cheaper Edition. Crown 8vo. Cloth, price 2s. 6d.

SENIOR (N. W.).

Alexis De Tocqueville. Correspondence and Conversations with Nassau W. Senior, from 1833 to 1859. Edited by M. C. M. Simpson. 2 vols. Large post 8vo. Cloth, price 21s.

Seven Autumn Leaves from Fairyland. Illustrated with Nine Etchings. Square crown 8vo. Cloth, price 3s. 6d.

SHADWELL (Maj.-Gen.), C.B.

Mountain Warfare. Illustrated by the Campaign of 1799 in Switzerland. Being a Translation of the Swiss Narrative compiled from the Works of the Archduke Charles, Jomini, and others. Also of Notes by General H. Dufour on the Campaign of the Valtelline in 1635. With Appendix, Maps, and Introductory Remarks. Demy 8vo. Cloth, price 16s.

SHAKSPEARE (Charles).

Saint Paul at Athens : Spiritual Christianity in Relation to some Aspects of Modern Thought. Nine Sermons preached at St. Stephen's Church, Westbourne Park. With Preface by the Rev. Canon FARRAR. Crown 8vo. Cloth, price 5s.

SHAW (Major Wilkinson).

The Elements of Modern Tactics. Practically applied to English Formations. With Twenty-five Plates and Maps. S cond and cheaper Edition. Small crown 8vo. Cloth, price 9s.

*** The Second Volume of "Military Handbooks for Officers and Non-commissioned Officers." Edited by Lieut.-Col. C. B. Brackenbury, R.A., A.A.G.

SHAW (Flora L.).

Castle Blair : a Story of Youthful Lives. 2 vols. Crown 8vo. Cloth, gilt tops, price 12s. Also, an dition in one vol. Crown 8vo. 6s.

SHELLEY (Lady).

Shelley Memorials from Authentic Sources. With (now first printed) an Essay on Christianity by Percy Bysshe Shelley. With Portrait. Third Edition. Crown 8vo. Cloth, price 5s.

SHERMAN (Gen. W. T.).

Memoirs of General W. T. Sherman, Commander of the Federal Forces in the American Civil War. By Himself. 2 vols. With Map. Demy 8vo Cloth, price 24s. *Copyright English Edition.*

SHILLITO (Rev. Joseph).

Womanhood : its Duties, Temptations, and Privileges. A Book for Young Women. Second Edition. Crown 8vo. Price 3s. 6d.

SHIPLEY (Rev. Orby), M.A.

Principles of the Faith in Relation to Sin. Topics for Thought in Times of Retreat. Eleven Addresses. With an Introduction on the neglect of Dogmatic Theology in the Church of England, and a Postscript on his leaving the Church of England. Demy 8vo. Cloth, price 12s.

Church Tracts, or Studies in Modern Problems. By various Writers. 2 vols. Crown 8vo. Cloth, price 5s. each.

Sister Augustine, Superior of the Sisters of Charity at the St. Johannis Hospital at Bonn. Authorized Translation by Hans Tharau from the German Memorials of Amalie von Lasaulx. Second edition. Large crown 8vo. Cloth, price 7s. 6d.

SKINNER (James).

Coelestia : the Manual of St. Augustine. The Latin Text side by side with an English Interpretation, in 36 Odes, with Notes, and a plea *for the* Study *of* Mystic Theology. Large crown 8vo. Cloth, price 6s.

SMITH (Edward), M.D., LL.B., F.R.S.

Health and Disease, as In- fluenced by the Daily, Seasonal, and other Cyclical Changes in the Human System. A New Edition. Post 8vo. Cloth, price 7s. 6d.

Practical Dietary for Families, Schools, and the Labouring Classes. A New Edition. Post 8vo. Cloth, price 3s. 6d.

Tubercular Consumption in its Early and Remediable Stages. Second Edition. Crown 8vo. Cloth, price 6s.

Songs of Two Worlds. By
the Author of " The Epic of Hades."
Sixth Edition. Complete in one
Volume, with Portrait. Fcap. 8vo.
Cloth, price 7s. 6d.

Songs for Music.
By Four Friends. Square crown
8vo. Cloth, price 5s.
Containing songs by Reginald A.
Gatty, Stephen H. Gatty, Greville
J. Chester, and Juliana Ewing.

SPEDDING (James).
Reviews and Discussions,
Literary, Political, and His-
torical, not relating to Bacon.
Demy 8vo. Cloth, price 12s. 6d.

STAPFER (Paul).
Shakspeare and Classical
Antiquity : Greek and Latin Anti-
quity as presented in Shakspeare's
Plays. Translated by Emily J. Carey.
Large post 8vo. Cloth, price 12s.

St. Bernard on the Love
of God. Translated by Marianne
Caroline and Coventry Patmore.
Cloth extra, gilt top, price 4s. 6d.

STEDMAN (Edmund Clarence).
Lyrics and Idylls. With
other Poems. Crown 8vo. Cloth,
price 7s. 6d.

STEPHENS (Archibald John), LL.D.
The Folkestone Ritual
Case. The Substance of the Argument delivered before the Judicial
Committee of the Privy Council. On
behalf of the Respondents. Demy
8vo. Cloth, price 6s.

STEVENS (William).
The Truce of God, and other
Poems. Small crown 8vo. Cloth,
price 3s. 6d.

STEVENSON (Robert Louis).
Virginibus, Puerisque, and
other Papers. Crown 8vo. Cloth,
price 6s.

STEVENSON (Rev. W. F.).
Hymns for the Church and
Home. Selected and Edited by the
Rev. W. Fleming Stevenson.
The most complete Hymn Book
published.

STEVENSON (Rev. W. F.)—*continued*.
The Hymn Book consists of Three
Parts :—I. For Public Worship.—
II. For Family and Private Worship.
—III. For Children.
*** Published in various forms and
prices, the latter ranging from 8d.
to 6s. Lists and full particulars
will be furnished on application to
the Publishers.*

STOCKTON (Frank R.).
A Jolly Fellowship. With
20 Illustrations. Crown 8vo. Cloth,
price 5s.

STORR (Francis), and TURNER Hawes).
Canterbury Chimes ; or,
Chaucer Tales retold to Children.
With Illustrations from the Elles-
mere MS. Extra Fcap. 8vo. Cloth,
price 3s. 6d.

STRETTON (Hesba).
David Lloyd's Last Will.
With Four Illustrations. Royal
16mo., price 2s. 6d.

The Wonderful Life.
Thirteenth Thousand. Fcap. 8vo.
Cloth, price 2s. 6d.

Through a Needle's Eye :
a Story. Crown 8vo. Cloth, price
6s.

STUBBS (Lieut.-Colonel F. W.)
The Regiment of Bengal
Artillery. The History of its
Organization, Equipment, and War
Services. Compiled from Published
Works, Official Records, and various
Private Sources. With numerous
Maps and Illustrations. 2 vols.
Demy 8vo. Cloth, price 32s.

STUMM (Lieut. Hugo), German
Military Attaché to the Khivan Ex-
pedition.
Russia's advance East-
ward. Based on the Official Reports
of. Translated by Capt. C. E. H.
VINCENT. With Map. Crown 8vo.
Cloth, price 6s.

SULLY (James), M.A.
Sensation and Intuition.
Demy 8vo. Second Edition. Cloth,
price 10s. 6d.

Pessimism : a History and
a Criticism. Demy 8vo. Price 14s.

Sunnyland Stories.
By the Author of "Aunt Mary's Bran Pie." Illustrated. Small 8vo. Cloth, price 3s. 6d

Sweet Silvery Sayings of
Shakespeare. Crown 8vo. Cloth gilt, price 7s. 6d.

SYME (David).
Outlines of an Industrial
Science. Second Edition. Crown 8vo. Cloth, price 6s.

Tales from Ariosto. Retold for
Children, by a Lady. With three illustrations. Crown 8vo. Cloth, price 4s. 6d.

TAYLOR (Algernon).
Guienne. Notes of an Autumn
Tour. Crown 8vo. Cloth, price 4s. 6d.

TAYLOR (Sir H.).
Works Complete. Author's
Edition, in 5 vols. Crown 8vo. Cloth, price 6s. each.
Vols. I. to III. containing the Poetical Works, Vols. IV. and V. the Prose Works.

TAYLOR (Col. Meadows), C.S.I., M.R.I.A.
A Noble Queen : a Romance
f Indian History. New Edition. With Frontispiece. Crown 8vo. oth. Price 6s.

Seeta. New Edition with
frontispiece. Crown 8vo. Cloth, price 6s.

Tippoo Sultaun : a Tale of
the Mysore War. New Edition with Frontispiece. Crown 8vo. Cloth, price 6s.

Ralph Darnell. New Edi-
tion. With Frontispiece. Crown 8vo. Cloth, price 6s.

The Confessions of a Thug.
New Edition. With Frontispiece. Crown 8vo. Cloth, price 6s.

Tara : a Mahratta Tale.
New Edition. With Frontispiece. Crown 8vo. Cloth, price 6s.

TENNYSON (Alfred).
The Imperial Library Edi-
tion. Complete in 7 vols. Demy 8vo. Cloth, price £3 13s. 6d. ; in Roxburgh binding, £4 7s. 6d.

TENNYSON (Alfred)—*continued*
Author's Edition. Complete
in 6 Volumes. Post 8vo. Cloth gilt ; or half-morocco, Roxburgh style :—

VOL. I. Early Poems, and English Idylls. Price 6s. ; Roxburgh, 7s. 6d.

VOL. II. Locksley Hall, Lucretius, and other Poems. Price 6s. ; Roxburgh, 7s. 6d.

VOL. III. The Idylls of the King (*Complete*). Price 7s. 6d.; Roxburgh, 9s.

VOL. IV. The Princess, and Maud. Price 6s.; Roxburgh, 7s. 6d.

VOL. V. Enoch Arden, and In Memoriam. Price 6s. ; Roxburgh, 7s. 6d.

VOL. VI. Dramas. Price 7s. ; Roxburgh, 8s. 6d.

Cabinet Edition. 12 vols.
Each with Frontispiece. Fcap. 8vo. Cloth, price 2s. 6d. each.

CABINET EDITION. 12 vols. Complete in handsome Ornamental Case. 32s.

The Royal Edition. With
25 Illustrations and Portrait. Cloth extra, bevelled boards, gilt leaves. Price 21s.

The Guinea Edition. Com-
plete in 12 vols., neatly bound and enclosed in box. Cloth, price 21s. French morocco or parchment, price 31s. 6d.

The Shilling Edition of the
Poetical and Dramatic Works, in 12 vols., pocket size. Price 1s. each.

The Crown Edition. Com-
plete in one vol., strongly bound in cloth, price 6s. Cloth, extra gilt leaves, price 7s. 6d. Roxburgh, half morocco, price 8s. 6d.

** Can also be had in a variety of other bindings.

TENNYSON (Alfred)—*continued.*

Original Editions :

Ballads and other Poems.
Fcap. 8vo. Cloth, price 5s.

The Lover's Tale. (Now for the first time published.) Fcap. 8vo. Cloth, 3s. 6d.

Poems. Small 8vo. Cloth, price 6s.

Maud, and other Poems. Small 8vo. Cloth, price 3s. 6d.

The Princess. Small 8vo. Cloth, price 3s. 6d.

Idylls of the King. Small 8vo. Cloth, price 5s.

Idylls of the King. Complete. Small 8vo. Cloth, price 6s.

The Holy Grail, and other Poems. Small 8vo. Cloth, price 4s. 6d.

Gareth and Lynette. Small 8vo. Cloth, price 3s.

Enoch Arden, &c. Small 8vo. Cloth, price 3s. 6d.

In Memoriam. Small 8vo. Cloth, price 4s.

Queen Mary. A Drama. New Edition. Crown 8vo. Cloth, price 6s.

Harold. A Drama. Crown 8vo. Cloth, price 6s.

Selections from Tennyson's Works. Super royal 16mo. Cloth, price 3s. 6d. Cloth gilt extra, price 4s.

Songs from Tennyson's Works. Super royal 16mo. Cloth extra, price 3s. 6d.
Also a cheap edition. 16mo. Cloth, price 2s. 6d.

Idylls of the King, and other Poems. Illustrated by Julia Margaret Cameron. 2 vols. Folio. Half-bound morocco, cloth sides, price £6 6s. each.

Tennyson for the Young and for Recitation. Specially arranged. Fcap. 8vo. Price 1s. 6d.

Tennyson Birthday Book. Edited by Emily Shakespear. 32mo. Cloth limp, 2s.; cloth extra, 3s.

** A superior edition, printed in red and black, on antique paper, specially prepared. Small crown 8vo. Cloth extra, gilt leaves, price 5s.; and in various calf and morocco bindings.

Songs Set to Music, by various Composers. Edited by W. G. Cusins. Dedicated by express permission to Her Majesty the Queen. Royal 4to. Cloth extra, gilt leaves, price 21s., or in half-morocco, price 25s.

An Index to "In Memoriam." Price 2s.

THOMAS (Moy).
A Fight for Life. With Frontispiece. Crown 8vo. Cloth, price 3s. 6d.

THOMPSON (Alice C.).
Preludes. A Volume of Poems. Illustrated by Elizabeth Thompson (Painter of "The Roll Call"). 8vo. Cloth, price 7s. 6d.

THOMSON (J. Turnbull).
Social Problems ; or, an Inquiry into the Law of Influences. With Diagrams. Demy 8vo. Cloth, price 10s. 6d.

THRING (Rev. Godfrey), B.A.
Hymns and Sacred Lyrics. Fcap. 8vo. Cloth, price 3s. 6d.

TODHUNTER (Dr. J.)
A Study of Shelley. Crown 8vo. Cloth, price 7s.

Alcestis : A Dramatic Poem. Extra fcap. 8vo. Cloth, price 5s.

Laurella ; and other Poems. Crown 8vo. Cloth, price 6s. 6d.

Translations from Dante, Petrarch, Michael Angelo, and Vittoria Colonna. Fcap. 8vo. Cloth, price 7s. 6d.

TURNER (Rev. C. Tennyson).
Sonnets, Lyrics, and Translations. Crown 8vo. Cloth, price 4s. 6d.

TURNER (Rev. C. Tennyson)—
continued.

Collected Sonnets, Old and
New. With Prefatory Poem by Alfred
Tennyson; also some Marginal Notes
by S. T. Coleridge, and a Critical
Essay by James Spedding. Fcap.
8vo. Cloth, price 7s. 6d.

TWINING (Louisa).

Recollections of Work-
house Visiting and Management during twenty-five years.
Small crown 8vo. Cloth, price 3s. 6d.

UPTON (Major R. D.).

Gleanings from the Desert
of Arabia. Large post 8vo. Cloth,
price 10s. 6d.

VAUGHAN (H. Halford), some-
time Regius Professor of Modern
History in Oxford University.

New Readings and Ren-
derings of Shakespeare's Tra-
gedies. 2 vols. Demy 8vo. Cloth,
price 25s.

VILLARI (Prof.).

Niccolo Machiavelli and
His Times. Translated by Linda
Villari. 2 vols. Large post 8vo.
Cloth, price 24s.

VINCENT (Capt. C. E. H.).

Elementary Military
Geography, Reconnoitring, and
Sketching. Compiled for Non-
Commissioned Officers and Soldiers
of all Arms. Square crown 8vo.
Cloth, price 2s. 6d.

VYNER (Lady Mary).

Every day a Portion.
Adapted from the Bible and the
Prayer Book, for the Private Devo-
tions of those living in Widowhood.
Collected and edited by Lady Mary
Vyner. Square crown 8vo. Cloth
extra, price 5s.

WALDSTEIN (Charles), Ph. D.

The Balance of Emotion
and Intellect: An Essay Introductory to the Study of Philosophy.
Crown 8vo. Cloth, price 6s.

WALLER (Rev. C. B.)

The Apocalypse, Reviewed
under the Light of the Doctrine of
the Unfolding Ages and the Resti-
tution of all Things. Demy 8vo.
Cloth, price 12s.

WALTERS (Sophia Lydia).

The Brook: A Poem. Small
crown 8vo. Cloth, price 3s. 6d.

A Dreamer's Sketch Book.
With Twenty-one Illustrations by
Percival Skelton, R. P. Leitch,
W. H. J. Boot, and T. R. Pritchett.
Engraved by J. D. Cooper. Fcap.
4to. Cloth, price 12s. 6d.

WATERFIELD, W.

Hymns for Holy Days and
Seasons. 32mo. Cloth, price 1s. 6d.

WATSON (William).

The Prince's Quest and
other Poems. Crown 8vo. Cloth,
price 5s.

WATSON (Sir Thomas), Bart.,
M.D.

The Abolition of Zymotic
Diseases, and of other similar ene-
mies of Mankind. Small crown 8vo.
Cloth, price 3s. 6d.

WAY (A.), M.A.

The Odes of Horace Lite-
rally Translated in Metre. Fcap.
8vo. Cloth, price 2s.

WEBSTER (Augusta).

Disguises. A Drama. Small
crown 8vo. Cloth, price 5s.

WEDMORE (Frederick).

The Masters of Genre
Painting. With sixteen illustrations.
Large crown 8vo. Cloth, price
7s. 6d.

Wet Days, by a Farmer.
Small crown 8vo. Cloth, price 6s.

WHEWELL (William), D.D.

His Life and Selections
from his Correspondence. By
Mrs. Stair Douglas. With Portrait
from a Painting by Samuel Laurence.
Demy 8vo. Cloth, price 21s.

WHITAKER (Florence).

Christy's Inheritance. A
London Story. Illustrated. Royal
16mo. Cloth, price 1s. 6d.

WHITE (A. D.), LL.D.

Warfare of Science. With
Prefatory Note by Professor Tyndall.
Second Edition. Crown 8vo. Cloth,
price 3s. 6d.

WHITNEY (Prof. W. D.)
Essentials of English
Grammar for the Use of Schools.
Crown 8vo. Cloth, price 3s. 6d.

WICKSTEED (P. H.).
Dante : Six Sermons. Crown
8vo. Cloth, price 5s.

WILKINS (William).
Songs of Study. Crown 8vo.
Cloth, price 6s.

WILLIAMS (Rowland), D.D.
Stray Thoughts from the
Note-Books of the Late Rowland Williams, D.D. Edited by
his Widow. Crown 8vo. Cloth,
price 3s. 6d.

Psalms, Litanies, Coun-
sels and Collects for Devout
Persons. Edited by his Widow.
New and Popular Edition. Crown
8vo. Cloth, price 3s. 6d.

WILLIS (R.), M.D.
Servetus and Calvin : a
Study of an Important Epoch in the
Early History of the Reformation.
8vo. Cloth, price 16s.

William Harvey. A History
of the Discovery of the Circula-
tion of the Blood. With a Portrait
of Harvey, after Faithorne. Demy
8vo. Cloth, price 14s.

WILLOUGHBY(The Hon. Mrs.).
On the North Wind —
Thistledown. A Volume of Poems.
Elegantly bound. Small crown 8vo.
Cloth, price 7s. 6d.

WILSON (Erasmus).
Egypt of the Past. With
Chromo-lithographs and numerous
Illustrations in the Text. Crown
8vo. Cloth.

WILSON (H. Schütz).
The Tower and Scaffold.
A Miniature Monograph. Large
fcap. 8vo. Price 1s.

Within Sound of the Sea.
By the Author of " Blue Roses,"
"Vera," &c. Third Edition. 2 vols.
Crown 8vo. Cloth, gilt tops, price
12s.
*** Also a cheaper edition in one
vol. with frontispiece. Price 6s.

WOLLSTONECRAFT (Mary).
Letters to Imlay. With a
Preparatory Memoir by C. Kegan
Paul, and two Portraits in *eau forte*
by Anna Lea Merritt. Crown 8vo.
Cloth, price 6s.

WOLTMANN (Dr. Alfred), and
WOERMANN (Dr. Karl).
History of Painting in An-
tiquity and the Middle Ages.
Edited by Sidney Colvin. With nu-
merous illustrations. Medium 8vo.
Cloth, price 28s. ; cloth, bevelled
boards, gilt leaves, price 30s.

WOOD (Major-General J. Creigh-
ton).
Doubling the Consonant.
Small crown 8vo. Cloth, price 1s. 6d.

WOODS (James Chapman).
A Child of the People,
and other poems. Small crown 8vo.
Cloth, price 5s.

Word was made Flesh.
Short Family Readings on the
Epistles for each Sunday of the
Christian Year. Demy 8vo. Cloth,
price 10s. 6d.

WRIGHT (Rev. David), M.A.
Waiting for the Light, and
other Sermons. Crown 8vo. Cloth,
price 6s.

YOUMANS (Eliza A.).
An Essay on the Culture
of the Observing Powers of
Children, especially in connection
with the Study of Botany. Edited,
with Notes and a Supplement, by
Joseph Payne, F.C.P., Author of
"Lectures on the Science and Art of
Education," &c. Crown 8vo. Cloth,
price 2s. 6d.

First Book of Botany.
Designed to Cultivate the Observing
Powers of Children. With 300 Engravings. New and Cheaper Edition. Crown 8vo. Cloth, price 2s. 6d.

YOUMANS (Edward L.), M.D.
A Class Book of Chemistry,
on the Basis of the New System.
With 200 Illustrations. Crown 8vo.
Cloth, price 5s.

YOUNG (William).
Gottlob, etcetera. Small
crown 8vo. Cloth, price 3s. 6d.